Best of the Best Presents

Bob Warden's
Favorite Recipes
for cook's essentials® Cookware

skillet italian chicken pot pie...p187

Best of the Best Presents

Bob Warden's Favorite Recipes

for cook's essentials® Cookware

by Robert Warden

with Ronda DiGuglielmo and Donna Land

QUAIL RIDGE PRESS

Preserving America's Food Heritage

ISBN 978-1-934193-87-7

First Edition

Printed in USA

Authors:
Robert Warden

with Ronda DiGuglielmo
and Donna Land

Author Photograph© Benoit Cortet

Food Photography:
Alison Miksch
On the cover: Peach Pouch Pie with Blueberries, page 147

Design:
Laura Wright

Published by:
Quail Ridge Press and Great Chefs International

QUAIL RIDGE PRESS
Preserving America's Food Heritage

www.quailridge.com
www.greatchefsinternational.com

contents

sausage, sage and apple skillet stuffing...p69

foreword by Gwen McKee

As a cookbook author and editor, I have seen a whole lot of cookbooks that I would rate everywhere from absolutely outstanding to positively dull. Here is one by Bob Warden that goes to the top of the absolutely outstanding chart. I am so pleased to be introducing a cookbook that I not only endorse, but highly recommend.

Several years ago, Bob and I co-authored a **cook's essentials**® cookbook together that was a huge success—and a barrel of fun. This time he flew solo, but oh my, he must love flying, because in my opinion, this book soars!

I'll tell you something about my friend Bob—he is never boring. Whether we're in Pennsylvania or Mississippi, or otherwise emailing, messaging, or talking on the phone, Bob and I have been kitchen buddies exchanging ideas for a lot of years—fifteen, I think. We both love preparing and enjoying good food, and consider it our mission to share our many years of cooking expertise with everybody who enjoys good food—which sometimes translates to "anybody who will listen." Well, when Bob talks, I listen. And in this lovely cookbook especially, you get the chance to listen with me.

Bob Warden and Gwen McKee on the set at QVC

I always enjoy tossing ideas around with Bob. If he thinks it's a good one, he makes it happen. In the late 90s, he helped to develop **cook's essentials** cookware, and people all over the world are glad he did—and that most assuredly includes me. Not long ago, it was brought up that all of us who own **cook's essentials** cookware need Bob's expertise on how to best utilize those lovely pots and pans. And, in his usual cheery manner, he quickly responded, "Okay, let's do it." And, heavenly days—after an extensive development process—here it is!

This cookbook offers unique cooking experiences:

- Did you know you could make a cherry pie in a skillet? Indeed, you can.

- Want to try Buffalo Corn on the Cob in your skillet? (We're not talking boiled here.)

- Have you ever made chicken pot pie in anything but a pie or casserole dish? You guessed it . . . get out your skillet. (Well, it sounds to me like pot pie should be made in a pot of some kind.)

- And Pineapple Upside-Down Cake without a cake pan—right in the skillet? Oh yeah.

As a bonus, you'll be washing one less vessel. We like that. And, no surprise, Bob has produced a whole book of recipes that will allow you to utilize your cookware in more and better ways, so that it will also, in a matter of speaking, make your cookware sing! He has also included incredible photography, extra "Tips," and "A Word from Bob" notes that give additional suggestions, reminders, and embellishments—it all adds up to one beautiful, usable cookbook.

I recommend you read through all these recipes, especially the creative "7 Ways, 7 Days" chapter that suggests seven variations for seven family favorite recipes. Try a few that intrigue you. You'll soon have your own favorites and you'll get some new ideas in the process.

Once again, I am so proud to put Quail Ridge Press' "Best of the Best" seal of approval on a Bob Warden cookbook. Cooking out of it is like putting your feet under his table at suppertime—and that is a very nice thing indeed.

Gwen McKee

Gwen McKee is a cookbook publisher, author, editor, and frequent QVC guest. Her company, Quail Ridge Press, has published over 200 cookbooks.

introduction

cook it fast, cook it well

Somewhere along the line, the idea emerged that it's impossible to eat well if you live the way Americans do today. Demands on our time and attention are so extreme, this notion goes, that any given meal is likely to be a compromise or an afterthought.

Well, I don't believe it. It's true that most of us are constantly out of time. No matter. There is an alternative to settling for one rushed, sub-par meal after another. It's about knowing the right shortcuts, the ones that save time without getting in the way of good results.

With a little help in learning and using those timesaving techniques, anyone can turn out great-tasting, nutritious dishes without spending hours in the kitchen.

Welcome to the *Bob Warden's Favorite Recipes for cook's essentials® Cookware*, a collection of ideas, recipes and kitchen tips that was put together expressly to help every busy cook save time, simplify kitchen work and serve delightful meals.

I developed this book as a companion piece to QVC's outstanding, exclusive **cook's essentials** line of premium cookware. If you're going to make the most of the techniques that this book suggests, you'll want to have the proper equipment. That doesn't have to be **cook's essentials**, of course. Good recipes can work well with any well-designed, well-made cookware.

Still, our line was innovated and manufactured to give cooks what they need for practically any kitchen work. And the selection of recipes I provide here assumes that readers will have a complete set of the good equipment they need.

I've heard people say that a great cook can make wonderful food without the benefit of first-class cookware. (It's the kind of statement some folks are bound to direct your way when you spend time as a TV spokesperson for first-class cookware.)

Just an opinion, now, but I think that's wrong. I'll say more about this later, but my point of view is that the right tools make any job easier.

In any case, when you use *Bob Warden's Favorite Recipes for cook's essentials® Cookware*, you'll find that your prep time, satisfaction and mealtime enjoyment sky-rocket, while time and labor you put into preparing meals plummet. That's a pledge from me to you.

some basics about this cookbook

First of all, it's important to let you know that every recipe you'll find here was carefully and thoroughly tested in real kitchen conditions. The information you see on times, temperatures, quantities and methods is reliable. Stick with it, and you'll be gratified by your success. Grow beyond it, adding your own special variations and extras to your favorite entries, and you'll be even more pleased.

I've included a Pantry List to help you stock up on the staples you'll find repeatedly on these pages. (Of course, if your pantry contains these basic items, you'll have what you need to cook almost anything, so the value of the list goes far beyond this book.)

The actual recipes are constructed to streamline your kitchen efforts. Header information shows how much prep and cook time you'll need, and how many the recipe serves. The Shopping List for each one tells you the amounts you'll need of all ingredients, and lists them in the order in which they're used. Directions are clear, complete and to the point. You don't need to be an expert cook to use this reference. Prove it to yourself by tackling a recipe chosen at random.

Many of the entries conclude with a tip that suggests ways to switch ingredients for an interesting flavor twist. Other tips tell you how to shave even more time off the preparation.

In truth, speed and convenience are built into all our recipes. Wherever it was possible to save time and not sacrifice quality, the shortcut was the path I took. For instance, look at the Pineapple Upside-Down Cake on page 178. Instead of baking the cake separately, this recipe saves a step by having you put the cake batter right on top of the pineapple slices in the bottom of the pan.

As important as the speed factor was in selecting and developing these recipes, it never became the first consideration. That was always the excellence of the finished food. I hope you're as excited to try these great recipes out as I am to share them with you.

7 ways, 7 days

From the beginning, a big part of what I had in mind for this book was to help people find welcome shortcuts in cooking—not timesavers that produce barely adequate stuff no one likes much, but quick and easy ways to make really great meals happen.

I've found a lot of ways to push that idea forward, but I had the most fun with chapter seven—fittingly called "7 Ways, 7 Days."

This all started when I considered what it would take to revitalize and rejuvenate some of the most familiar recipes in anybody's cooking repertoire.

Every one of us has a few standard dishes that turn up on our tables often—I hesitate to call them favorites, because that may not be the way we really react to them. These are entrées, sides and desserts that we return to time and time again, the well-worn selections of the table.

It's not that these recipes are terrible or useless. We resort to them so often because they do some worthwhile things for us. From experience, we know how to cook them, so we're confident we can make them quickly and reasonably well. Anytime we think about making them, there's a good chance all the ingredients we need will be on hand in the pantry and the refrigerator. And we're also sure we have all the cookware and utensils it will take to put them on the table.

All that is on the plus side. There's only one serious weakness: we may already have cooked and served a dish like this 147 times. So at this point, it's not much fun to eat . . . or to prepare, for that matter. The idea of going for number 148 doesn't inspire much excitement.

What if I figured out new treatments for a septet of the most familiar, tried-and-true dishes—no, I won't say worn-out—that Americans eat? And what if I considered every one of them in a new light, trying to invent some fresh and appealing takes on them? Finally, what if I gave each one seven new faces, enough so a cook can try one every day of the week, without a single repetition?

I came up with seven old warhorses that everyone knows very well:

Chicken Pot Pie

Corn on the Cob

Omelets

Green Bean Casserole

Chicken and Rice

Pineapple Upside-Down Cake

. . . and the ever-popular king of them all, Macaroni and Cheese!

It's easy to forget that dishes like these are classics for a reason. At the heart of each one is good food, enjoyable flavor and texture and manageable preparation and cooking time.

Any new takes on these dishes would have to honor these standout characteristics. No doubt it would be possible to work up terrific, elaborate versions of each one while stretching out the pantry-to-table time by hours. But what would be the point of that? Unless the new recipes were both good and fast, no one would be interested in them.

That was the mandate. With a little help from some chef/developer friends, I set out to see what could be done. The idea was never to try something out of the ordinary for its own sake. At the same time, we never shied away from a combination just because it was new and original. Our research has produced some spectacular new ideas,

though. It's been a hoot to see where the whole premise led.

Flip to the Contents on page 5, and you'll get a quick idea about that. In the mood for a delicious change from your usual chicken pot pie? Try tonight's entry with dumplings (page 186), cheese-herb biscuit topping (page 186), or biscuit bites (page 185). Try it Italian- or Mexican-style (pages 187 and 188, respectively). Or sample the lollapalooza Ultimate Skillet Chicken Pot Pie (page 189), rich in vegetables and amped up with a tot of brandy.

We're just getting started here. From other classics, we spin off Green Bean and Tomato Casserole with Whole-Grain Crunch Topping (page 192), Baked Cornbread, Chicken and Rice (page 196), the Puffy Seafood Scampi Omelet (page 175), spicy Thai Corn on the Cob (page 163) and the fun-to-say, easy-to-love Peach Pouch Pie with Blueberries (page 147).

In particular, I direct your attention to the recipe that shatters forever any notion that macaroni and cheese is the champion of boring comfort foods. Give our aptly-named OMG Lobster Mac 'n' Cheese (page 167) a try, and see if you ever think about macaroni and cheese the same way again.

"7 Ways, 7 Days" features exactly 49 recipes. If you didn't want to eat anything else, you could enjoy these recipes for weeks without repeating yourself.

Prefer to spread them further across the calendar? You'll have plenty to look forward to for a long time to come. As promised, they are all delicious, all fast and all planned perfectly to complement our **cook's essentials** cookware.

six courses

The first six chapters of the book are dedicated to a slightly more conventional cookbook presentation—one chapter each for Appetizers, Soups and Salads, Side Dishes, Main Dishes, Brunch and Desserts.

The recipes are anything but conventional. They are carefully calibrated to provide the perfect balance between the quality of the dish and the speed of its preparation.

Here's a quick rundown of what you can expect from each section.

APPETIZERS

The recipes here are among the very fastest to prepare in the whole book—and among the very easiest to prepare properly. You'll find them appropriately light, but with great savor and texture that make them really memorable. We call them appetizers; many of these entries also make excellent party fare. In particular, we recommend the Mini Citrus Crab Cakes with Herbed Vinaigrette (page 34), Spinach-and-Sausage-Stuffed Mushrooms (page 25) and Warm French Onion Dip (page 22) as treats your party guests will enjoy.

SOUPS AND SALADS

Many of the recipes in this section incorporate a Mediterranean flair—check out the Caesar Steak Sandwich Salad (page 53), Tuscan Chicken and White Bean Soup (page 39) and Mediterranean Couscous Salad, with tender chicken over romaine lettuce (page 63). Some draw on the full-flavored traditions of the Southwest; others are new takes on familiar American classics. Though they're great as accompaniments, you'll find that most of them work well as stand-alone lunches or lighter dinners, too.

SIDE DISHES

The emphasis here is on variety—and on a melding of flavors that truly complements a range of main courses. My testers were knocked out by the taste and texture of the Sausage, Sage and Apple Skillet Stuffing (page 69), the creamy Pecorino Skillet-Baked Risotto with Wild Mushrooms (page 74), and the versatile Sweet Potato Pancakes (page 67). It's always a subtle trick to find side dishes that "belong" with the rest of what's on the plate—I think this selection will match up beautifully with dishes in this cookbook . . . and others, too.

MAIN DISHES

Whatever you favor as the underlying staple for a hearty main course, you'll find examples here that are destined to become favorites. Take a whack at our Pork Tenderloin with Dried Cherry Port Sauce (page 110), Burgundy Braised Beef with Onions and Mushrooms, (page 109) and Easy Pasta Puttanesca (page 106), the delectable dinner with the saucy name. By the way, I find that when cooks are concerned about how long it will take to prepare a dish, they worry most about the entrée. Be confident in these selections. We made a special effort to plan every one of them to fit well into your busy schedule.

BRUNCH

When you rise a little late for whatever reason, you want the first meal of the day to pack a little extra punch—something beyond the toast-and-coffee blandness of an ordinary breakfast. Some of the recipes in this section deliver eye-opening tastes and mouth-filling textures. Don't miss the Spiced Apple Puffed Pancakes (page 115), the surprising Cheese

Blintz Casserole with Blueberries (page 117) and the special Huevos Rancheros (page 129), ideal when you have a little time to linger over a great morning meal. I've also included a spritz of great drinks, with or without a light touch of spirits, whichever you prefer, to start the day just right.

DESSERTS

For those who think this should have been first in the sequence, your patience is about to be rewarded. You don't have to be a chocolate fiend to enjoy this selection—but it helps. The Maple Peanut Butter Chocolate Chip Cookies (page 143) are unique. The Tiramisù Eggnog Parfaits (page 154) are remarkable. And the Caramel Pear Cherry Almond Tarts (page 148) are amazing—you'll probably find them to be like nothing you've ever had before. Don't be intimidated, as some cooks are, when you confront a dessert recipe for the first time. These entries are calibrated to be gratifyingly quick and easy.

The entries we've cited here and many more are waiting for your attention. Start now—why delay pleasures like these?

about cook's essentials— the right stuff in the kitchen

This cookbook is intended for anyone who can benefit from sound ideas in food preparation, with a special emphasis on speed and convenience. Its recipes are meant to help busy people stay on track through their crazy, jam-packed days—without sacrificing the quality of their meals or their nutritive value.

To say it the simplest way possible, I prepared this book for everyone in America who cooks. Really, you could also say I did it for everyone who eats. It's true, though, that I had it very much in mind to create a book that would have special value for the smart consumers who use the **cook's essentials** line of cookware from QVC.

As such, this book was planned and the recipes were developed in ways that would enable people to get the most from their **cook's essentials** collections. That's not in any way to say this cookbook is only for **cook's essentials** users—but only to point out that it was purpose-created as a companion piece to the line. If you use other products, following the recipes you'll find here will work out just fine.

how cook's essentials came to be

It might be a good idea to explain the genesis of the **cook's essentials** concept. A very specific set of circumstances produced this breakthrough line, and it definitely has affected the way people think about cookware.

In 1998, QVC had been an established marketing power for more than a decade, and was providing consumers with all sorts of products that embodied the channel's motto of quality, value and convenience. When it came to cookware, though, there was an issue.

It was difficult—impossible, really—to find a "name" manufacturer at the time willing to provide the highest quality cookware at prices that could work for QVC's discriminating audience. The only way we could devise to provide both superior quality and that expected level of value (including a lifetime guarantee) was to develop our own cookware line, and manufacture it through a private label agreement with a respected maker.

Naturally, convenience is also at the heart of things today. We saw savvy cooks looking for every opportunity to save time, making meals that delivered good eating fast. But if you were stuck scrubbing a pile of pots and pans with cooked-on gunk afterward, you really hadn't made any headway at all. So the **cook's essentials** line had to be nonstick cookware.

Well, it worked. We were able to produce a line that was better than almost anything else consumers could buy—but without attaching an unreasonable price tag. Very soon **cook's essentials** products—premium, lifetime-warranted cookware at the cost of throwaways—were in hundreds of thousands of homes coast-to-coast.

And the lifetime guarantee didn't stifle the line's growth as you might expect. New buyers kept calling in, responding to a rapidly developing reputation. As our customers experienced what we had to offer, they wanted to supplement their basic collections with additional equipment. These satisfied buyers became repeat customers for new **cook's essentials** offerings. What's more, they recognized that our cookware provided great gift choices—excellent quality made the cookware worth giving, and outstanding value made it worth buying.

From the start, the idea was to make **cook's essentials** the line to trust when you wanted to set up as a successful cook. It would emphasize what people really needed to make things happen fast and well in the kitchen. It would not try to out-gadget the gadgeteers, and it would not extend the line to items too specialized to be helpful to large numbers of cooks.

the revolution in nonstick technology

Along came the middle part of the first decade of this century, and the revolutionary DuPont nonstick coatings that were a longtime **cook's essentials** hallmark were no longer the same powerful selling point they'd been before. We were on the lookout for the technological basis to produce a major upgrade to the line—and in the last few years it finally arrived.

Any nonstick coating works at the most basic level by providing a porous surface that foods won't adhere to. The difficulty with stainless steel cookware has always been this: Its surface doesn't readily accept a coating that provides the needed porosity. It took the inspiration and expertise of wizard metallurgists and chemists to develop a rugged new ceramic alternative that actually incorporates steel into the coating.

Not only does this innovation work like a charm to prevent cooked foods from sticking, it has also made the surfaces more incredibly durable than ever, even when you use metal utensils. Tests on our earlier-generation cooking surfaces showed that they would last through 200,000 cook-and-cleanup cycles. If you used a pan three times a day every day, it would take you 182 years to use it 200,000 times—which is why we could offer a lifetime guarantee without hesitation.

The new generation of PFOA-free nonsticks will survive one million cook-and-clean cycles. That makes a **cook's essentials** pan as much an heirloom as a kitchen tool.

the longer view of cook's essentials

No matter how good a nonstick surface might be, it takes a lot more than that to make an excellent line of cookware.

One truly essential element is appearance. I know there are cooks—and some of them are distinguished chefs—who take pride in making truly wonderful food out of the nastiest-looking, most battered, clunkiest pots and pans you've ever seen. For most of us, it's a little different. The pride we feel in our cooking abilities is mirrored and reinforced by our pride in the tools we use when we exercise those abilities. I really believe that better-looking cookware makes many of us better cooks.

Myself, I pick up a handsome, well-designed pot with anticipation. It seems right for the job I have in mind. It makes me want to get cooking. If it's made to please the hand as well as the eye, so much the better—and all **cook's essentials** products are designed with good ergonomics in mind. When a kitchen tool of any kind feels awkward, you'll discover that cooking with it is less of a pleasure and more of a chore.

Remember also that a great-looking pot or pan can save you a step—that's the one where you have to swap what you've made over to a presentable serving dish. These vessels look fine on the table. You can feel good about serving right out of them, and you'll have one less dish to clean up afterward. In fact, you may even need less extra serving stuff in the cupboard, which is a benefit both in the space you conserve and in the money you save by having to buy less serving ware.

Another thing that's essential is good construction. Pick up any of our cookware, and you'll notice the heft right away. It feels solid, because it is. This is serious kitchen equipment, manufactured with an attention to detail that makes it last longer and work more effectively. It's not only that it resists damage because of its construction, though it certainly does. Thick sides and bottoms also contribute to more even distribution of heat. And that means better cooking results.

Versatility is essential for sure. This is expressed first of all in the various materials in which the line is available—stainless steel with clear or solid lids, porcelain-enameled aluminum, hard-anodized aluminum, all-clad stainless. This enables the experienced cook to select the variety that works best with the kind of cooking he or she does. Novices can choose any of the lines in full confidence that whatever they select will perform up to expectations—permanently.

Versatility is something we play up in this cookbook. If you're equipped with kitchen tools from the **cook's essentials** line, you'll have just what you need to produce stellar results, no matter what you're attempting. In truth, excellent results with these recipes are also within reach if you use any other pots and pans—we never intended to make this book useful only to customers who own only our cookware.

No matter what equipment you use to prepare these recipes, I'm confident that you'll be pleased with the results. To get the full value of the book, try as many as you can over the course of a few weeks or months. You'll quickly start to amass a list of favorites. And you'll soon be as happy with the eating pleasure you get from these dishes as you are with the convenience they offer.

carbonara fondue...p20

appetizers

We all like to have a "little something" before we eat our meal, or to have on hand for entertaining family and friends. In this chapter you can use some shortcut techniques to prepare great appetizers with flair, trendy flavors, and the time to enjoy them with your guests.

A food processor is a terrific timesaver. Try Tuscan Kale and White Bean Toasts, and you can choose how smooth (or chunky) you want the dip to be—simply adjust the time and speed of processing.

Make the Warm French Onion Dip, and you will have a rich, dense onion flavor—onion soup mix does that trick, all without a teary eye in sight. Another very flavorful convenience is a jar of roasted red peppers—just drain and dice, and your Roasted Red Pepper Dip is nearly ready to serve.

Did you ever make flatbread with pizza dough? Better yet, have you bought the dough to make it? Now available in many grocery stores, pizza dough is either frozen in the freezer case, or defrosted in the refrigerator case for you to take home, ready to start Flatbread with Roasted Eggplant and Peppers. Another place to buy the dough is your local pizza shop—just smile as you ask if they will sell you some.

Check your store for other prepared ingredients that will get you out of the kitchen fast to start the party!

A word from Bob...

Pick up a rotisserie chicken at the grocery for cooked chicken ready to go—add to nachos, dips, spreads, even as a substitute for the sausage in the Spinach-and-Sausage-Stuffed Mushrooms!

carbonara fondue

Prep: 15 min.   **Cook:** 20 min.   **Serves:** 6

SHOPPING LIST
6 slices bacon
2 garlic cloves, minced
3 tablespoons chopped green onions,
  divided
1 cup Alfredo sauce
½ cup dry white wine
2 cups shredded Gruyère cheese
1 loaf baguette, sliced or cubed

1) Cook bacon in a 10-inch nonstick skillet over medium heat, turning occasionally until crisp. Remove from skillet, reserving 2 tablespoons drippings in skillet. Drain bacon on paper towels. Cool, and chop.

2) Add garlic to drippings, and cook for about 1 minute over medium heat, stirring frequently (do not brown). Add 2 tablespoons onions. Cook for about 2 minutes or until softened, stirring occasionally.

3) Stir in Alfredo sauce and wine, and mix well. Reduce heat to low, and add cheese, stirring occasionally until cheese is melted. Stir in bacon, and transfer to fondue pot. Top with remaining onions.

4) Serve with sliced bread.

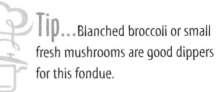

Tip...Blanched broccoli or small fresh mushrooms are good dippers for this fondue.

cowboy fondue

Prep: 15 min.   **Cook:** 15 min.   **Serves:** 10

SHOPPING LIST
1 tablespoon olive oil
1 onion, chopped (about 1 cup)
1 medium green bell pepper, chopped (about 1 cup)
½ pound chopped ham steak
1 (16-ounce) package Velveeta® cheese, cubed
1 (14½-ounce) can diced tomatoes, undrained
1 baguette loaf, cubed

1) Heat oil in a 2½-quart nonstick saucepan over medium heat. Add
   onion and pepper. Cook about 3 minutes or until tender-crisp, stirring
   occasionally.

2) Add ham, and cook until heated through.

3) Add cheese and tomatoes, and heat until cheese is melted and bubbly,
   stirring occasionally.

4) Serve with bread cubes, cornbread cubes, blue corn chips or red bell pepper strips for
   dipping.

A word from Bob...

Other vegetables make great additional dippers: cauliflower, mushrooms, broccoli and even French fries!

Tip...Leftover cooked ham can be used instead of the ham steak.

roasted red pepper dip

Prep: 15 min.   **Cook:** 15 min.   **Serves:** 16

SHOPPING LIST

1 (8-ounce) package cream cheese, softened
2 cups mayonnaise
2 cups shredded mozzarella cheese
1 (12-ounce) jar roasted red peppers, drained, and diced
1 tablespoon dried minced onion
2 slices cooked bacon, crumbled
Fresh vegetables, baguette slices and pretzel crisps for dipping

1) Place cream cheese and mayonnaise in a 1½-quart nonstick pan, and stir until well blended.

2) Add cheese, peppers, onion and bacon. Heat over medium heat until cheese is melted and bubbly.

3) Pour into serving dish. Serve with fresh vegetables, bread, and crisps.

Tip...This dip is delicious warm or at room temperature. If not served immediately, cover and refrigerate until ready to serve. Bring to room temperature or heat gently.

warm french onion dip

Prep: 15 min.   **Cook:** 15 min.   **Serves:** 8

SHOPPING LIST

1 (16-ounce) container sour cream
½ cup mayonnaise
2 cups shredded Swiss cheese
1 (1-ounce) envelope French onion soup mix
3 tablespoons chopped sun-dried tomatoes
4 tablespoons thinly sliced green onions, divided
1 round bread loaf

1) Combine sour cream, mayonnaise, cheese, and soup mix in a 1½-quart nonstick saucepan. Heat over medium heat until heated through. Stir in sun-dried tomatoes, and 3 tablespoons onions.

2) Cut a circle in the bread loaf to make a bowl; remove, cube, and reserve bread. Transfer cheese mixture into bread bowl, and serve immediately. Garnish with remaining onions.

3) Serve with reserved bread cubes.

Tip...Add cooked and crumbled bacon.

peach goat cheese dip

Prep: 10 min.   **Cook:** 15 min.   **Serves:** 12

SHOPPING LIST

1 (8-ounce) package cream cheese, softened
8 ounces goat cheese, softened
1 cup peach mango salsa
¼ teaspoon ground cinnamon
1 tablespoon minced jalapeño
1½ teaspoons butter
½ cup panko bread crumbs
Pita chips

1) Heat cheeses in 1½-quart nonstick saucepan over medium heat until creamy and smooth.

2) Stir in salsa, cinnamon and jalapeño. Heat until heated through, stirring frequently.

3) Melt butter in an 8-inch nonstick skillet over medium heat. Add bread crumbs, stirring frequently until toasted.

4) Transfer cheese mixture to 9-inch pie plate. Top with bread crumbs, and serve with pita chips.

A word from Bob...

If there is any left over, this dip makes a wonderful sandwich spread for turkey or chicken on toasted bread.

Tip...This dip can be reheated in the oven. For a spicier dip, use plain peach salsa, and add a few drops of hot sauce.

spinach-and-sausage-stuffed mushrooms

Prep: 15 min.   **Cook:** 30 min.   **Makes:** about 4 dozen

SHOPPING LIST

3 sweet or hot Italian sausage links, casings removed (about 10 ounces)
2 garlic cloves, minced
4 (10-ounce) packages white or baby bella mushroom caps (½ cup mushroom stems removed and chopped)
1 (10-ounce) package frozen chopped spinach, thawed, and squeezed dry
½ cup panko or fresh bread crumbs
½ cup shredded Parmesan cheese, divided
Kosher salt and freshly ground pepper to taste

1) Break sausage into small pieces, and place in 10-inch skillet. Cook for 5–6 minutes over medium heat or until cooked through. Add garlic and mushroom stems. Cook for 4–5 minutes or until mushroom stems are cooked through. Add spinach, bread crumbs and ¼ cup cheese. Stir to blend. Season with salt and pepper.

2) Preheat oven to 375°.

3) Stuff the mushroom caps with sausage mixture. Place them on a lightly greased, rimmed baking sheet. Sprinkle with remaining cheese.

4) Bake in preheated oven for 20–25 minutes or until mushrooms are softened.

 Tip...Use extra mushroom stems in a salad, slicing them, if very large.

flatbread with roasted eggplant and peppers

Prep: 10 min.   **Cook:** 45 min.   **Makes:** 4 cups

SHOPPING LIST
1 tablespoon olive oil
1 medium onion, diced (1½ cups)
2 garlic cloves, minced
1 medium eggplant (about 1½ pounds), diced (6 cups)
1 red bell pepper, diced (1½ cups)
¾ cup prepared pasta sauce
½ teaspoon red pepper flakes
2 tablespoons julienned fresh basil
Salt and pepper to taste
2 pounds refrigerated or frozen pizza dough, thawed, if frozen

1) Heat oil in 8-quart sauté pan over medium heat. Add onion, and cook for 3–4 minutes or until softened. Add garlic, eggplant, bell pepper, sauce and pepper flakes.

2) Cover, and cook over low heat for 30–40 minutes or until eggplant is tender, stirring occasionally. Season with basil, salt and pepper.

3) Divide each pound of dough into 4 pieces. Shape each piece into a round about 6 inches across. Heat a 10-inch sauté pan over medium-high heat. Place one dough round in the pan, and cook for 5–6 minutes on each side or until lightly golden. Repeat with remaining dough rounds. Cut or break the flatbread into wedges to serve.

4) Serve eggplant mixture warm, cold or at room temperature with the warmed flatbreads.

 Tip...Freshly prepared pizza dough can often be found at the grocery store. Most pizzerias will sell you the dough by the pound. To save time, you can also substitute naan flatbread or pocketless pita. Any remaining eggplant can be refrigerated and tossed over pasta, or enjoyed as a sandwich spread with fresh mozzarella on ciabatta bread.

aïoli with crispy potatoes

Prep: 10 min.   **Cook:** 45 min.
Makes: 28

SHOPPING LIST
14 new red potatoes (about 1½ pounds)
1 head garlic
¼ cup olive oil, divided
Salt and pepper to taste
½ cup mayonnaise
2 tablespoons lemon juice

1) Place potatoes in 5-quart stockpot, and cover with water. Bring to a boil, then reduce heat, and simmer for 20 minutes or until potatoes are tender. Drain, and cool.

2) Preheat oven to 400°. Cut the top off the garlic head, and place it in 7-inch oven-proof skillet. Drizzle with 1 tablespoon oil. Cook at 400° for 35–40 minutes or until garlic is tender and golden. Cool. Squeeze garlic into a bowl; add any oil remaining in the skillet. Add mayonnaise and lemon juice, and mix well.

3) Cut potatoes in halves (or quarters, if too large). Pour remaining oil in 5-quart stockpot, and add potatoes, cut sides down. Cook for 15–20 minutes over medium heat or until cut sides are golden and crisp. Sprinkle with salt and pepper.

4) Serve the potatoes warm with the roasted garlic mixture.

caramelized apple and onion tartlets

Prep: 15 min. **Cook:** 40 min.
Makes: 18 tartlets

SHOPPING LIST
2 tablespoons olive oil
1 small onion, diced (¾ cup)
1 large or 2 small Granny Smith apples,
  peeled, cored and diced (1½ cups)
1 teaspoon minced fresh thyme or
  rosemary
Kosher salt and freshly ground black pepper
  to taste
½ (17.3-ounce) package puff pastry sheets
  (1 sheet), thawed
2 ounces grated Gruyère cheese
  (about ½ cup)

1) Heat oil in 3-quart sauté pan over me-
    dium heat. Add onion and apples, and
    cook 20 minutes or until soft and cara-
    melized. Season with thyme or rosemary,
    salt and pepper. Cool.

2) Preheat oven to 400°. Line a baking
    sheet with parchment paper.

3) Unwrap, and unfold the puff pastry on
    a floured surface. Cut dough into thirds
    along the fold lines, creating 3 equal
    pieces. Cut each strip into 3 squares,
    then cut each square diagonally into
    triangles, making 18 triangles. Place
    them on a baking sheet. Spoon about
    2 teaspoons of apple mixture onto each
    triangle. Sprinkle cheese on top.

4) Bake at 400° for 15–20 minutes or until
    pastry is golden. Serve warm.

goat cheese-stuffed dates with bacon and balsamic glaze

Prep: 20 min.   **Cook:** 45 min.   **Serves:** 10

SHOPPING LIST
30 pitted dates (about 8 ounces)
4 ounces goat cheese
16 slices bacon, each cut in half horizontally (about 1 pound)
½ cup balsamic vinegar

1) Preheat oven to 375°. Slit the side of each date, taking care not to split the date in half. Place ½ teaspoon goat cheese into each date, and pinch it closed. Roll ½ piece of bacon around each, and place on wire rack over a rimmed baking sheet.

2) Bake for 15–20 minutes at 375° or until bacon is cooked to desired doneness.

3) Place vinegar in 1½-quart saucepan, and bring to a boil. Simmer until reduced to 2 or 3 tablespoons. Drizzle over the dates when they come out of the oven.

4) Cool slightly, and serve.

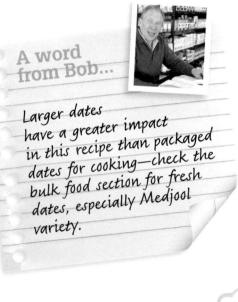

A word from Bob...

Larger dates have a greater impact in this recipe than packaged dates for cooking—check the bulk food section for fresh dates, especially Medjool variety.

Tip... The stuffed dates can be assembled in advance and held in the refrigerator. Let stand at room temperature 5 minutes before baking.

steak crostini with horseradish sauce

Prep: 10 min. **Cook:** 15 min. **Serves:** 6

SHOPPING LIST
2 tablespoons olive oil
Kosher salt and pepper to taste
1 Flat Iron steak (about 1½ pounds)
1 cup sour cream
2 tablespoons horseradish sauce
Cracked black pepper to taste
2 baguettes, thinly sliced
Fresh chopped parsley

1) Preheat oven to 400°.

2) Rub oil on both sides of the steak. Season with salt and pepper. Heat the sauté pan on medium-high heat. Add the steak. Sear until well browned on both sides. Place pan in preheated oven, and roast for 8–10 minutes or until desired doneness is reached. Cover loosely with foil, and let rest for 10 minutes.

3) Combine sour cream, sauce, and pepper in a medium bowl.

4) Thinly slice beef when ready to serve. Top each bread slice with ½ teaspoon sauce, a slice of beef, another small measure of sauce and a sprinkle of parsley.

 Tip...For rare beef, cook to an internal temperature of 125°. For medium rare, cook to 130°; for medium, cook to 135°. Have the bakery department slice the baguettes for you on the bread slicer in the store, saving time and ensuring even slices.

chicken fajita nachos

Prep: 15 min.   **Cook:** 10 min.   **Serves:** 20

SHOPPING LIST
1 tablespoon olive oil
1 small onion, diced (1 cup)
1 small green bell pepper, diced (1 cup)
1 small red bell pepper, diced (1 cup)
1 jalapeño pepper, diced (¼ cup)
1 garlic clove, minced
½ teaspoon chili powder
½ teaspoon ground cumin
2 cups shredded and chopped cooked chicken
Juice and zest of 1 lime
¼ cup chopped cilantro
1 (16-ounce) bag tortilla chips
1 ripe avocado, diced

1) Heat oil in 3-quart sauté pan over medium heat. Add onion and peppers. Cook for 4–5 minutes or until vegetables are tender-crisp. Add garlic, and cook another minute or until fragrant. Stir in chili powder and cumin. Add chicken, and heat through. Stir in lime juice, zest and cilantro.

2) Spread chips in a single layer on a serving tray. Spread chicken mixture evenly over chips, and top with avocado. Serve immediately.

 Tip...The chicken mixture can be made in advance and reheated when ready to serve. It can be halved easily for a smaller group.

tuscan kale and white bean toasts

Prep: 10 min. **Cook:** 10 min. **Serves:** 20

SHOPPING LIST
½ cup olive oil, divided
1 cup diced red onion
1 garlic clove, minced
4 cups shredded kale
1 (15-ounce) can small white beans, drained, and rinsed
1 tablespoon red wine vinegar
2 tablespoons shredded Parmesan cheese
Salt and pepper to taste
1 baguette, thinly sliced, and toasted

1) Heat 1 tablespoon oil in 3-quart sauté pan. Add onion, and cook for 4–5 minutes or until tender, and translucent. Add garlic, and cook 1 minute or until fragrant. Stir in kale, and cook 3–4 minutes or until wilted. Stir in beans.

2) Transfer mixture to food processor fitted with a steel blade, and drizzle in vinegar and remaining oil. Process in short bursts until mixture is well blended, and as smooth as desired. Stir in cheese, and season with salt, and pepper.

3) Serve warm or at room temperature on baguette toasts or crackers.

 Tip...To make the toasts, have the bakery department in your grocery slice a baguette or two for you on their slicing machine. Place slices in a single layer on a cookie sheet, and brush lightly with olive oil. Season with salt and pepper, if desired. Bake in a preheated 375° oven for 12–15 minutes or until golden. Cool, and store in an airtight container or zipper storage bag.

mini citrus crab cakes with herbed vinaigrette dipping sauce

Prep: 20 min.   **Cook:** 20 min.   **Serves:** 25

SHOPPING LIST

Crab Cakes:

3 (6-ounce) cans fancy lump crab, well drained, cartilage removed

1 egg, lightly beaten

1 tablespoon Dijon mustard

1 teaspoon lemon zest

1 tablespoon lemon juice

Cracked black pepper to taste

¼ cup finely chopped red bell pepper

4 green onions, white and light green parts trimmed, and thinly sliced (about ¼ cup)

1 cup fresh bread crumbs, divided

¼ cup olive oil, divided

Citrus Vinaigrette:

2 tablespoons lemon juice

1 tablespoon Dijon mustard

¼ cup olive oil

2 tablespoons mayonnaise

1 tablespoon fresh chopped parsley or chives

1) Combine crab, egg, mustard, lemon zest and juice, black pepper, bell pepper, onions and ½ cup bread crumbs in medium bowl.

2) Place remaining bread crumbs in shallow pie plate. Form crab mixture into cakes using a tablespoon measure or small ice cream scoop. Coat each crab cake in the bread crumbs.

3) Heat 1 tablespoon oil in 10-inch skillet or 3-quart sauté pan. Add crab cakes 7 or 8 at a time. Cook for 3 or 4 minutes per side or until golden. Transfer to a cookie sheet, and repeat with remaining oil and crab cakes.

4) Whisk together lemon juice, mustard, oil, mayonnaise and parsley.

5) Serve crab cakes warm with the Citrus Vinaigrette.

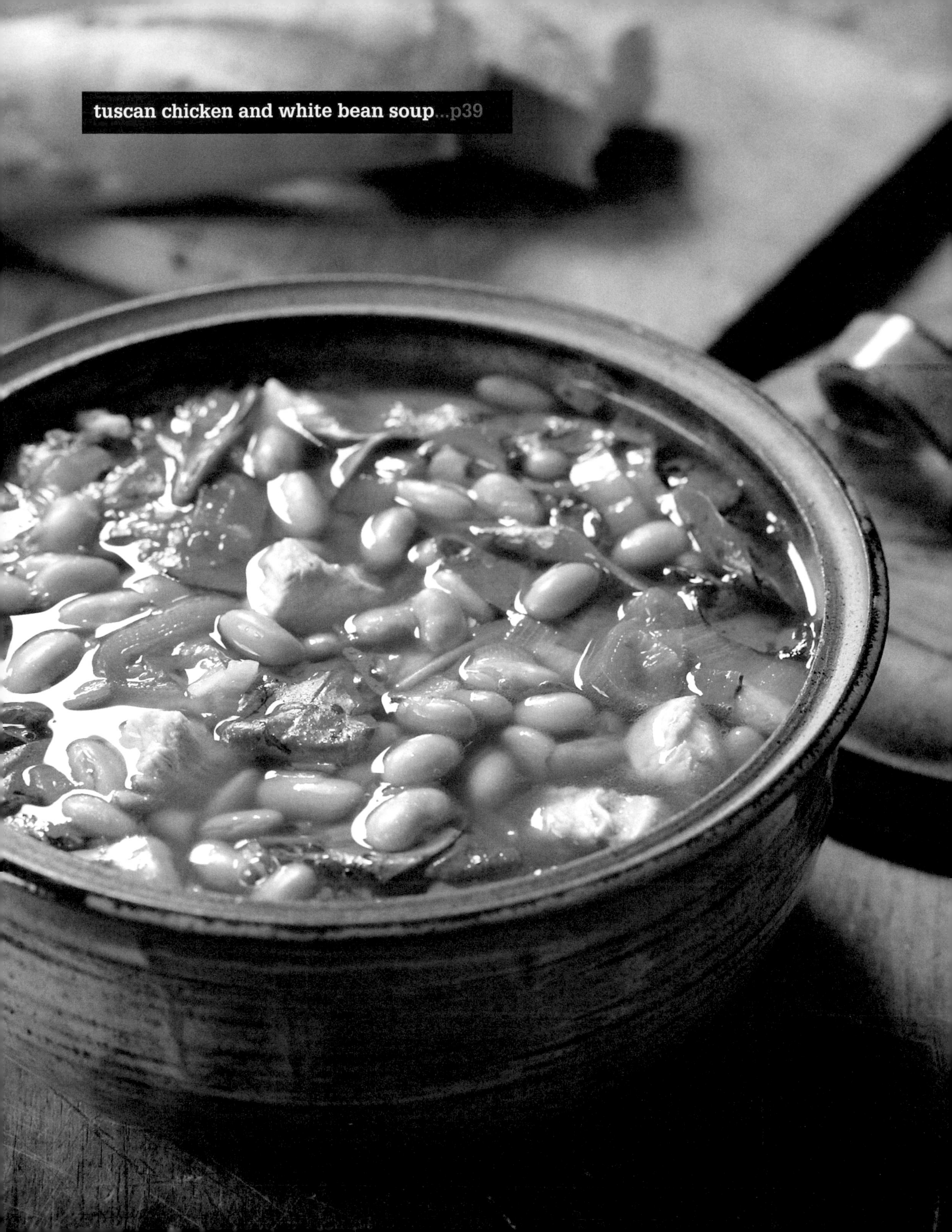
tuscan chicken and white bean soup...p39

soups & salads

Soups can be hearty enough for a meal or light enough to serve as its beginning, and we have many for you to enjoy in this chapter. They can each be prepared quickly, with ingredients you already have on hand, or can be more elaborate with freshly prepared vegetables, and simmered slowly for flavors to develop.

One key ingredient for successful soups is to start with flavorful stock or broth. Preparation does not have to be time consuming, though, and today's market offers many soup staples in a form that saves you the work. Look for chopped onions in the produce department or the freezer case. Chopped garlic is handy in jars found in the produce department as well.

Check the freezer for vegetables that were packed at their flavor peak—notably corn as used in Creamy Southwestern Bean Soup with Cornbread Croutons, and Shrimp, Scallop and Corn Chowder. You may also be fortunate enough to find the cooked cornbread in the bakery department.

Salads do not always have to be cold—savor our Sautéed Radicchio with Blue Cheese and Pistachios, as well as the Sautéed Peaches with Goat Cheese over Greens. Be sure to take advantage of the ever-present bagged and boxed greens at the grocery store, all washed and ready for you to serve at home. Talk about a timesaver!

A word from Bob...

Make enough soup for several days, and freeze in individual servings for a quick lunch another day.

tuscan chicken and white bean soup...p39

quick and easy chicken noodle soup

Prep: 20 min. **Cook:** 40 min. **Serves:** 6

SHOPPING LIST

1 tablespoon plus 1 teaspoon olive oil, divided
1½ pounds boneless, skinless chicken breasts, cut into ¾-inch pieces
4 carrots, sliced (about 2 cups)
2 stalks celery, sliced (about 1 cup)
1 small onion, chopped (about ½ cup)
½ teaspoon salt
6 cups water
2 tablespoons concentrated chicken broth
1 (14½-ounce) can diced tomatoes, undrained
6 sprigs parsley
1 bay leaf
8 ounces mini pasta, cooked according to package directions

1) Heat 1 tablespoon olive oil over medium-high heat in 6-quart stockpot. Add chicken. Cook chicken in batches, about 10 minutes or until browned, stirring occasionally.

2) Add remaining 1 teaspoon olive oil to pot. Add carrots, celery, onion, and salt. Cook 5 minutes, until vegetables are tender-crisp. Return chicken to pot, and add water, broth, tomatoes with their juice, parsley and bay leaf. Bring to a boil. Reduce heat to medium low, cover, and simmer 25 minutes or until chicken is cooked and vegetables are tender.

3) Stir pasta into soup, and serve.

tuscan chicken and white bean soup

Prep: 15 min. **Cook:** 35 min. **Serves:** 6

SHOPPING LIST

1 tablespoon olive oil
1½ pounds boneless, skinless chicken breasts, cut in 1-inch cubes
1 teaspoon salt
3 leeks, sliced, rinsed and drained (about 1 cup), or 1 onion, sliced
3 garlic cloves, chopped
6 cups water
2 tablespoons concentrated chicken stock
2 (15-ounce) cans cannellini beans, drained and rinsed
1 (7-ounce) package baby spinach

1) Heat olive oil over medium-high heat in 6-quart saucepot. Brown chicken with salt in 2 batches. Transfer to a medium bowl, and keep warm.

2) Add leeks to the saucepot, and cook over medium heat 3 minutes or until wilted. Add garlic, and cook 1 minute or until fragrant. Add water and stock, and bring to a boil. Return chicken to saucepot. Simmer covered for 20 minutes or until leeks are tender.

3) Stir in beans and spinach. Cook 2 minutes or until beans are heated through and spinach wilts.

 **Tip...** Be sure to clean leeks thoroughly by cutting in half lengthwise, then rinsing between each of the leaves carefully to remove dirt.

smokey lentil soup

Prep: 15 min. **Cook:** 37 min. **Serves:** 16

SHOPPING LIST
2 tablespoons olive oil
1 large onion, chopped (about 1 cup)
3 carrots, chopped (about 1 cup)
3 stalks celery, chopped (about 1 cup)
1 teaspoon salt
3 garlic cloves, chopped
1 tablespoon cumin
1 tablespoon smoked paprika
1½ teaspoons oregano
8 cups water
3 tablespoons concentrated vegetable broth
1 (28-ounce) can diced tomatoes, undrained
1 (1-pound) package red lentils

1) Heat olive oil over medium heat in 6-quart stockpot. Add onion, carrots, celery, and salt. Cook 6 minutes, or until vegetables begin to soften, stirring occasionally.

2) Stir in garlic, cumin, paprika, and oregano, and cook 1 minute.

3) Stir in water, broth, tomatoes and lentils, and bring to a boil over high heat. Reduce heat to medium low, and simmer, covered, 30 minutes or until lentils and vegetables are tender. If soup is too thick, add additional water and broth.

chicken pozole

Prep: 10 min. **Cook:** 1 hour **Serves:** 6

SHOPPING LIST
1 tablespoon vegetable oil
1½ pounds boneless, skinless chicken thighs
½ teaspoon salt
1 small onion, chopped
3 garlic cloves, chopped
2 tablespoons tomato paste
1 teaspoon cumin
1 teaspoon oregano
6 cups water
3 tablespoons concentrated chicken broth
2 (15-ounce) cans hominy, drained
2 tablespoons chopped fresh cilantro
Lime wedges

1) Heat vegetable oil in 6-quart stockpot over medium-high heat. Season chicken with salt, and cook 10 minutes or until browned; transfer to platter and keep warm.

2) Add onion to stockpot, and cook 3 minutes. Add garlic, tomato paste, cumin, and oregano, and cook 1 minute.

3) Add water, broth, and chicken. Bring to a boil. Reduce heat to medium low, and simmer, covered, 30 minutes or until chicken is tender. Transfer chicken to cutting board, and shred. Return chicken to pot, and stir in hominy. Simmer 15 minutes. Stir in cilantro, and serve with lime wedges.

creamy southwestern bean soup with cornbread croutons

Prep: 10 min.   **Cook:** 30 min.   **Serves:** 8

SHOPPING LIST

2 tablespoons vegetable oil
1 medium onion, chopped
1 teaspoon salt
2 garlic cloves, minced
1 tablespoon cumin
2 teaspoons chili powder
½ teaspoon ancho chili powder
1 (28-ounce) can diced tomatoes, undrained
4 cups water
2 tablespoons concentrated vegetable broth
1 (15-ounce) can black beans, rinsed and drained
1 (15-ounce) can kidney beans, rinsed and drained
1 (15-ounce) cans chick peas, rinsed and drained
1 (15-ounce) can corn, drained
1 (8-ounce) carton sour cream
2 tablespoons chopped fresh cilantro
4 cups cubed cornbread
2 tablespoons butter, divided

1) Heat vegetable oil over medium heat in a 6-quart stockpot. Add onion and salt, and cook 5 minutes, stirring occasionally. Add garlic, cumin, and chili powders, and cook 1 minute. Stir in tomatoes, water, broth, beans and corn. Bring to a boil. Reduce heat to medium low, and simmer 20 minutes. Stir in sour cream and cilantro.

2) Serve with cornbread croutons, made by melting 1 tablespoon butter in 10-inch skillet. Add half of cornbread, and cook over medium-high heat for 6 minutes or until cornbread is browned and crisp, stirring frequently. Repeat with remaining 1 tablespoon butter and remaining cornbread.

 Tip…Substitute any beans you have on hand—small white beans, cannellini beans, pinto beans or any of your favorites.

spicy gazpacho

Prep: 20 min.   **Chill:** 6 hours   **Serves:** 6

SHOPPING LIST
2 pounds ripe tomatoes, coarsely chopped
1 green bell pepper, coarsely chopped
1 medium cucumber, peeled, seeded and diced
1 small onion, chopped
1 serrano chile or jalapeño pepper, seeded and chopped
3 garlic cloves
2 slices white bread, crusts removed and torn into pieces
3 tablespoons red wine vinegar
3 tablespoons olive oil
1 teaspoon salt
Croutons and diced cucumber for garnish

1) Combine tomatoes, bell pepper, cucumber, onion, serrano chile pepper, garlic, bread, vinegar, oil and salt. Purée in 2 batches in blender until smooth.

2) Chill 6 hours or overnight to allow flavors to blend.

3) Serve cold with croutons and diced cucumber for garnish.

 Tip...Try "Spiked Gazpacho." Add ½ cup vodka to mixture. Serve in shooters.

shrimp, scallop and corn chowder

Prep: 20 min.   **Cook:** 25 min.   **Serves:** 6

SHOPPING LIST

2 tablespoons butter

1 small onion, chopped

2 stalks celery, sliced

1 medium red bell pepper, seeded, and chopped

1 teaspoon salt

1 pound red potatoes, cut in ½ inch pieces

2 garlic cloves, minced

3 tablespoons flour

3 cups skim milk

2 cups water

1 tablespoon concentrated chicken or vegetable stock

1 teaspoon Old Bay Seasoning®

¾ pound shrimp, peeled, deveined, and coarsely chopped

¾ pound bay scallops

2 cups frozen corn, thawed

1 tablespoon chopped fresh thyme leaves

1) Melt butter in a 6-quart pot, and cook onion, celery, pepper and salt over medium heat for 5 minutes, stirring occasionally. Add potatoes and garlic, and cook for 5 minutes or until potatoes are almost tender, stirring occasionally.

2) Stir in flour, and cook for 2 minutes, stirring frequently. Stir in milk, water, stock and seasoning. Bring to a boil over high heat. Reduce heat to low, and simmer chowder for 5 minutes or until vegetables are tender. Add shrimp, scallops and corn. Reduce heat to low, and simmer 5 minutes or until shrimp turn pink. Stir in thyme.

 **Tip**...For richer seafood flavor, replace water and concentrated stock with homemade stock. Reserve shrimp shells, and place them with 4 cups water in a saucepan. Add any vegetable scraps from the recipe preparation, including onion peel and celery leaves, tops or bottoms. Add 1 or 2 whole, unpeeled garlic cloves, 10 peppercorns, 1 bay leaf and 1 teaspoon salt. Bring to a boil, reduce heat and simmer uncovered for at least 30 minutes. The longer the stock simmers, the more flavor it will have. Strain solids, and reserve stock.

mushroom and quinoa soup with herbs

Prep: 10 min.   **Cook:** 45 min.   **Serves:** 8

SHOPPING LIST

2 tablespoons butter
1 medium onion, chopped (about 1 cup)
2 carrots, chopped (about ½ cup)
2 stalks celery, chopped (about ½ cup)
½ teaspoon salt
3 (8-ounce) packages sliced mushrooms (combination of white, cremini, shiitake)
2 garlic cloves, chopped
6 cups water
2 tablespoons concentrated vegetable broth
½ cup red quinoa, rinsed
1 tablespoon chopped fresh parsley
1 tablespoon chopped fresh sage
1 tablespoon chopped fresh thyme

1) Melt butter in 6-quart stockpot over medium heat. Cook onion, carrots, celery and salt for 5 minutes, until vegetables begin to soften, stirring occasionally. Add mushrooms and garlic, and cook 5 minutes, until vegetables are tender-crisp, stirring occasionally.

2) Add water and broth, and bring to a boil. Reduce heat to medium low, and simmer for 15 minutes.

3) Stir in quinoa. Cook 20 minutes or until vegetables and quinoa are tender. Stir in parsley, sage and thyme.

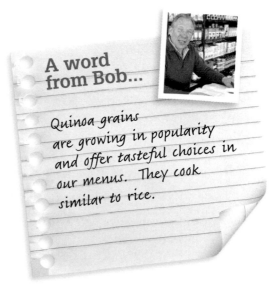

A word from Bob...

Quinoa grains are growing in popularity and offer tasteful choices in our menus. They cook similar to rice.

caldo verde

Prep: 10 min.   **Cook:** 40 min.   **Serves:** 6

SHOPPING LIST

2 pounds potatoes, peeled and cut into chunks
1 large onion, chopped
3 garlic cloves, chopped
1 teaspoons salt
12 ounces chorizo
6 cups water
2 tablespoons concentrated chicken broth
2 cups finely shredded kale

1) Combine potatoes, onion, garlic, salt, chorizo, water, and broth in 6-quart saucepot. Leave chorizo whole. Bring to a boil. Reduce heat to medium low, and simmer 30 minutes, or until potatoes are tender.

2) Transfer chorizo to cutting board, slice thinly and reserve. Transfer potato mixture to food processor or blender, and purée in batches until smooth. Transfer soup to pot, and add kale. Bring to a boil, and simmer 5 minutes or until kale until is wilted. Adjust salt, if necessary.

3) Ladle soup into bowls, and garnish each with chorizo slices.

 **Tip...** It's especially easy to purée the soup with an immersion, or handheld, blender that purées right in the original saucepot.

thai chicken salad

Prep: 20 min. **Cook:** 25 min. **Serves:** 6

SHOPPING LIST
1½ pounds boneless, skinless chicken breast halves
2 cups water
4 slices lime
4 sprigs cilantro
2 garlic cloves, minced
½ teaspoon salt
½ cup rice wine vinegar
2 tablespoons lime juice
3 tablespoons Thai seasoning sauce (fish sauce)
2 tablespoons sweet chili sauce
2 cups shredded Napa cabbage
½ cup shredded carrots
½ cup julienned radish
¼ cup coarsely chopped cilantro

1) Combine chicken, water, lime, cilantro, garlic and salt in 2-quart saucepan. Bring to boil over medium-high heat. Reduce heat to low, and simmer covered for 25–30 minutes, until chicken is tender and cooked through. Transfer chicken to cutting board, shred and set aside.

2) Combine vinegar, lime juice, seasoning sauce and chili sauce in a large bowl. Stir in shredded chicken, cabbage, carrots, radish and cilantro.

 Tip... Serve as a salad ,or wrap in Bibb lettuce leaves.

chicken caesar salad with parmesan cheese crisps

Prep: 15 min. **Cook:** 30 min. **Serves:** 6

SHOPPING LIST

1 cup shredded Parmesan cheese, divided
1½ pounds boneless, skinless chicken breast halves, sliced into ½-inch-thick strips
1 tablespoon olive oil
1 garlic clove, pressed
½ teaspoon lemon zest
½ teaspoon salt
¼ teaspoon freshly grated pepper
1 head romaine lettuce, torn into bite-sized pieces
½ cup Easy Caesar Dressing (page 53)
1 cup croutons

Cheese Crisps:

1) Sprinkle 3 tablespoons cheese to form a 3-inch circle in 10-inch nonstick skillet sprayed with nonstick cooking spray. Cook over medium heat for 2 minutes or until cheese is golden; turn and cook 30 seconds.

2) Transfer to paper towels to cool. Repeat with remaining cheese to make 6 crisps.

Salad:

1) Combine chicken, oil, garlic, lemon zest, salt, and pepper in medium bowl. Brown chicken in 2 batches in 10-inch skillet until cooked through. Remove, and cool slightly.

2) Toss romaine with dressing; arrange on serving platter. Top with chicken, croutons and Cheese Crisps.

shrimp and avocado caesar salad in tortilla bowls

Prep: 20 min. **Cook:** 10 min. **Serves:** 4

SHOPPING LIST

4 (8-inch) flour tortillas
1 tablespoon mayonnaise
½ avocado, mashed
2 tablespoons plus 1 tablespoon lime juice, divided
2 tablespoons olive oil
2 garlic cloves, plus 1 garlic clove, pressed, divided
2 tablespoons grated Parmesan cheese
½ teaspoon anchovy paste
1 pound shrimp, peeled and deveined
¼ teaspoon chipotle chili powder
6 cups shredded romaine lettuce

1) Place tortilla in a bowl, forming it to shape of bowl. Place small glass dish in the center to weigh the tortilla down. Place bowl in microwave, and cook on HIGH, 1 minute. Let stand about 1 minute to harden. Transfer from bowl, and repeat with remaining tortillas.

2) Combine mayonnaise, avocado, 2 tablespoons lime juice, oil, 2 garlic cloves, cheese, and anchovy paste in a mini food processor, and process until smooth. Set aside.

3) Combine shrimp with remaining 1 tablespoon lime juice, remaining 1 pressed garlic clove, and chipotle chili powder. Cook in a 10-inch skillet over medium-high heat 6 minutes or until shrimp are no longer pink.

4) Toss romaine with dressing; divide evenly among tortilla bowls. Top with shrimp.

caesar steak sandwich salad

Prep: 10 min. **Cook:** 12 min.
Serves: 4

SHOPPING LIST
1 pound skirt steak, sliced into ½-inch strips
1 garlic clove, pressed
1 teaspoon Worcestershire sauce
½ teaspoon salt
1 teaspoon olive oil
4 cups thinly sliced romaine lettuce
3 tablespoons Easy Caesar Dressing
   (opposite)
4 slices Texas toast, prepared according to
   package directions
½ cup shredded Parmesan cheese

1) Combine steak, garlic, sauce and salt.
   Heat olive oil in 10-inch skillet over medium-high heat. Cook steak in 2 batches
   until desired doneness. Transfer to platter, and keep warm.

2) Toss lettuce with dressing. Arrange toast
   on platter. Top with cooked steak (pour
   any juices from steak over top) and lettuce. Sprinkle with cheese.

easy caesar dressing

Prep: 5 min. **Makes:** about 1 cup

SHOPPING LIST
½ cup mayonnaise
¼ cup grated Parmesan cheese
3 tablespoons olive oil
2 garlic cloves, pressed
1 tablespoon lemon juice
1 teaspoon Worcestershire sauce
1 teaspoon Dijon mustard
½ teaspoon anchovy paste
¼ teaspoon pepper

1) Whisk mayonnaise, cheese, oil, garlic,
   lemon juice, sauce, mustard, anchovy
   paste and pepper in a small bowl.

2) Refrigerate in a sealed container.

A word from Bob...

Using mayonnaise replaces the need to use raw egg yolks to prepare this classic dressing.

—53

garden salad with green goddess dressing

Prep: 10 min.   **Makes:** 1½ cups

SHOPPING LIST
½ cup mayonnaise
½ cup nonfat plain Greek yogurt
½ avocado
¼ cup chopped basil
¼ cup chopped parsley
1 tablespoon lemon juice
1 tablespoon olive oil
2 garlic cloves
2 green onions, coarsely chopped
1 teaspoon anchovy paste
1 head Boston lettuce, torn
2 tomatoes, sliced, then halved

1) Combine mayonnaise, yogurt, avocado, basil, parsley, lemon juice, oil, garlic, onions and anchovy paste in a food processor or mini chopper. Process until smooth.

2) Serve with lettuce and tomatoes.

cobb salad

Prep: 25 min.   **Serves:** 6

SHOPPING LIST
½ teaspoon Dijon mustard
¼ cup red wine vinegar
1 teaspoon Worcestershire sauce
1 garlic clove, crushed
¼ teaspoon salt
½ teaspoon freshly ground black pepper
⅓ cup olive oil
1 head romaine lettuce, coarsely chopped
2 ounces blue cheese, crumbled
6 strips cooked bacon, chopped
3 hard-boiled eggs, peeled and coarsely chopped
2 medium tomatoes, chopped
4 cups cooked chicken breast, cut into ½-inch cubes
1 avocado, peeled, pitted and cut into ½-inch pieces

1) Combine mustard, vinegar, sauce, garlic, salt and pepper in a bowl. Gradually whisk in oil. Set aside.

2) On a large platter, arrange romaine lettuce. Arrange cheese, bacon, eggs, tomatoes, chicken and avocado on the greens in neat rows. Drizzle salad with dressing, and serve.

tomato with fresh mozzarella and balsamic vinaigrette

Prep: 15 min.   **Cook:** 20 min.   **Serves:** 4

SHOPPING LIST
2 tablespoons butter, divided
2 tablespoons chopped shallots
⅔ cup balsamic vinegar
2 tablespoons chopped fresh basil, divided
½ teaspoon brown sugar
4 cups salad greens
2 medium ripe tomatoes, sliced
8 ounces fresh mozzarella, grated

1) Melt 1 tablespoon butter in a 1-quart saucepan, and cook shallot for 3 minutes or until tender. Add vinegar and 1 tablespoon basil, and bring to a boil. Reduce heat to low, and simmer 15 minutes or until mixture is reduced by half. Stir in sugar and remaining 1 tablespoon butter.

2) Arrange greens on platter. Arrange tomatoes and mozzarella over greens, then pour balsamic mixture over all.

3) Garnish with remaining basil, and serve with crusty bread.

 Tip...The warm vinaigrette is also delicious over fresh greens, like spinach or leaf lettuce or as a dressing for roasted eggplant.

sautéed radicchio with blue cheese and pistachios

Prep: 10 min. **Cook:** 14 min. **Serves:** 8

SHOPPING LIST

4 slices bacon, chopped
2 heads radicchio, sliced (about 8 cups)
¾ teaspoon salt
1 small apple, peeled, cored and julienned
2 tablespoons balsamic vinegar
¼ cup unshelled pistachios, toasted, if desired
2 ounces crumbled blue cheese (about ¼ cup)

1) Cook bacon over medium heat in 10-inch sauté pan about 6 minutes until crisp. Transfer bacon pieces to paper towels and drain. Add radicchio and salt. Cook over medium heat 8 minutes or until radicchio is tender, stirring occasionally.

2) Toss radicchio with reserved bacon, apple and vinegar. Sprinkle with pistachios and cheese.

 Tip... For a vegetarian version, omit bacon, and sauté radicchio in 1 tablespoon olive oil.

sautéed peaches with goat cheese over greens

Prep: 10 min.   **Cook:** 6 min.   **Serves:** 4

SHOPPING LIST

1 tablespoon butter
2 large peaches, sliced (about 3 cups)
Pinch of salt
2 tablespoons brown sugar
3 tablespoons balsamic vinegar
6 cups salad greens
¼ cup sliced almonds, toasted
2 ounces goat cheese, crumbled

1) Melt butter in 10-inch skillet. Add peaches and salt. Cook over medium heat 4 minutes or until slightly softened, stirring occasionally. Add sugar and vinegar. Cook 2 minutes until thickened slightly and peaches are tender.

2) Arrange greens on platter. Top with peach mixture, almonds and goat cheese.

 Tip... Add cooked chicken or shrimp to make this a main dish. Consider other fruits instead of the peaches: apricots, pineapple, apples or pears.

chicken fajita salad

Prep: 15 min. **Cook:** 10 min. **Serves:** 6

SHOPPING LIST

1½ pounds boneless, skinless chicken breasts, cut in ½-inch strips
2 tablespoons tequila
4 tablespoons lime juice, divided
2 garlic cloves
½ teaspoon salt
½ cup ranch dressing
¼–½ teaspoon chipotle chili powder
2 tablespoons chopped fresh cilantro
1 (15-ounce) can black beans, rinsed and drained
1 (15-ounce) can chick peas, rinsed and drained
1 (15-ounce) can corn, drained
1 cup chopped tomato
1 tablespoon olive oil
1 head romaine lettuce, torn into bite-sized pieces
6 (8-inch) flour tortillas (optional)

1) Combine chicken, tequila, 2 tablespoons lime juice, garlic, and salt in medium bowl. Let stand 15 minutes.

2) Combine dressing, chili powder, remaining 2 tablespoons lime juice, and cilantro in a bowl; set aside.

3) Combine beans, chick peas, corn and tomato in a large bowl. Stir in 2 tablespoons dressing mixture.

4) Heat olive oil in a 10-inch skillet. Cook chicken in 2 batches until cooked through, about 5 minutes each batch.

5) Arrange lettuce on platter; top with bean mixture and chicken. Serve with remaining dressing. May serve with warm tortillas, if desired.

Tip...Add to the fajita flavor by mixing in grilled or sautéed red and green bell pepper strips.

prosecco poached pear salad with prosciutto

Prep: 15 min.   **Cook:** 20 min.   **Serves:** 6

SHOPPING LIST
2 cups Prosecco wine
Juice and zest from 1 orange (½ cup juice, 2 teaspoons zest)
3 tablespoons brown sugar
6 whole cloves
2 cinnamon sticks
3 pears, halved and cored
1 (7-ounce) package baby arugula
6 slices prosciutto
2 ounces shaved Parmesan cheese

1) Combine wine, orange juice and zest, sugar, cloves and cinnamon in 10-inch sauté pan. Bring to a boil over medium-high heat. Add pears, cut side down. Simmer covered for 20 minutes or until pears are tender. Cool.

2) Arrange arugula on platter. Roll each prosciutto slice and arrange over arugula, alternating with pears. Drizzle with wine sauce and top with cheese.

A word from Bob...

Prosecco is an Italian dry white sparkling wine gaining popularity as an alternative to champagne.

Tip... Try using champagne or white or red wine instead of Prosecco.

mediterranean couscous salad

Prep: 20 min. **Cook:** 12 min. **Serves:** 6

SHOPPING LIST

1½ pounds boneless chicken breasts, cut in 1-inch cubes
3 tablespoons olive oil, divided
2 garlic clove, chopped, divided
½ teaspoon dried oregano
¾ teaspoon plus ¼ teaspoon lemon zest, divided
¼ teaspoon salt
⅛ teaspoon pepper
2 tablespoons lemon juice
2 tablespoons chopped fresh oregano (or ½ teaspoon dried)
3 cups cooked couscous
1 medium cucumber, peeled, seeded and diced (about 1½ cups)
1 large tomato, chopped (about 1½ cups)
½ cup halved kalamata olives
½ cup chopped red onion
½ cup toasted pine nuts
4 ounces crumbled feta cheese (about ½ cup)
9 cups torn romaine lettuce

1) Toss chicken with 1 tablespoon oil, half of chopped garlic, oregano, ¼ teaspoon lemon zest, salt and pepper. Let stand about 10 minutes.

2) Combine remaining 2 tablespoons oil, remaining ¾ teaspoon lemon zest, lemon juice, oregano and remaining garlic.

3) Cook chicken in lemon-oil mixture in 2 batches over medium-high heat in 10-inch sauté pan until well browned and cooked through. Remove from skillet, and cool slightly.

4) Combine couscous, cucumber, tomato, olives, onion, and pine nuts in a large bowl. Add chicken and dressing. Toss to coat. Stir in cheese. Serve over lettuce.

 **Tip...** For a unique Mediterranean flavor, add 2 tablespoons chopped fresh mint.

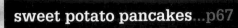
sweet potato pancakes...p67

side dishes

Today we are in the habit of not filling out our meals with side dishes, and we are missing something important. Not only is it better for us to have vegetables on our plate, many of these side dishes highly complement our main dish entrée. Change baked potatoes to Potato Pancakes, and watch your family sit up and take notice.

Adding extra flavor to these vegetables is pretty easy—stir in some chopped fresh herbs, dried seasonings, Dijon mustard (how about those Dijon Glazed Carrots?), pesto (Spaghetti Squash anyone?), or even hot sauce, and you have side dishes that will rival the main entrée.

You can save time in preparing side dishes, too. Don't peel the potatoes or peaches. Make side dishes in a nonstick skillet on top of the stove, and you don't have to heat up the oven. Cook the veggies first, then keep them warm while you make the sauce in the same skillet—one fewer pan to wash.

Resolve to add side dishes to your menu today by starting with the delectable ones in this chapter. Enjoy!

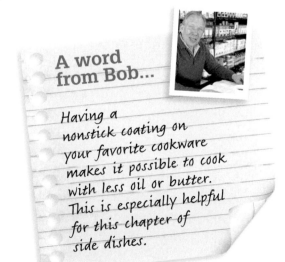

A word from Bob...

Having a nonstick coating on your favorite cookware makes it possible to cook with less oil or butter. This is especially helpful for this chapter of side dishes.

potato pancakes

Prep: 20 min. **Cook:** 8 min. **Serves:** 8

SHOPPING LIST

4 large potatoes, peeled (about 2 pounds), shredded
1 medium yellow onion, shredded (about 1 cup)
1 egg, beaten
1 teaspoon salt
½ teaspoon garlic powder
¼ teaspoon black pepper
2 tablespoons all-purpose flour
¼ cup canola oil

1) Squeeze liquid from potatoes and onions, and drain. Set aside. Combine egg, salt, garlic powder, pepper and flour in small bowl.

2) Heat oil in skillet over medium-high heat. Carefully place 4 (¼-cup) portions of potato mixture into hot oil. Immediately flatten with spatula to make ½-inch-thick pancakes. Cook 3 minutes each side or until golden brown, turning once. Transfer to paper-towel-lined plate. Repeat with remaining mixture.

3) Keep pancakes warm until serving time.

 **Tip**...Serve with applesauce or sour cream. Leftover pancakes can be reheated in a nonstick skillet for 2–3 minutes or until hot, turning over once.

sweet potato pancakes

Prep: 20 min.　**Cook:** 12 min.
Serves: 12

SHOPPING LIST
2 medium sweet potatoes (about 1½ pounds), peeled and grated
1 Granny Smith apple, unpeeled, cored and shredded
2 eggs, beaten
1 teaspoon salt
2 tablespoons brown sugar
½ teaspoon cinnamon
2 tablespoons all-purpose flour
¼ cup canola oil

1) Squeeze liquid from potatoes and apples, and drain. Set aside.

2) Combine eggs, salt, sugar, cinnamon, and flour in bowl. Heat oil in skillet over medium-high heat. Carefully place 4 (¼-cup) portions of potato mixture into hot oil. Immediately flatten with spatula to make ½-inch-thick pancakes. Cook 3 minutes each side, until golden brown. Transfer from oil to drain on paper-towel-lined plate. Repeat with remaining potato mixture.

3) Keep pancakes warm until served.

Tip…Serve with maple syrup and chopped pecans. Good alone for breakfast or brunch, these also are an excellent side dish for dinner.

sausage, sage and apple skillet stuffing

Prep: 8 min. **Cook:** 12 min. **Bake:** 40 min. **Serves:** 8

SHOPPING LIST
1 tablespoon canola oil
1 pound uncased Italian sweet sausage
1 onion, chopped (1 cup)
3 tablespoons sliced sage
3 garlic cloves, minced
6 tablespoons unsalted butter, divided
1 Granny Smith apple, peeled, cored and diced (1 cup)
1 tablespoon chicken concentrate
1⅓ cups water
4 cups cubed herb-seasoned stuffing
Salt and freshly ground black pepper to taste

1) Preheat oven to 350°.

2) Place canola oil and sausage in oven-proof (to 400°) 3-quart skillet over medium-high heat. Sauté 4–5 minutes, until almost browned.

3) Stir in onion and sage, and sauté 4 minutes or until onion is tender. Stir in garlic, and sauté 1–2 minutes, until fragrant. Fold in 4 tablespoons butter until melted. Remove from heat. Stir in apple.

4) Transfer to a large bowl. Stir in chicken concentrate, water and stuffing until well combined. Season lightly with salt and pepper. Return to skillet. Top with remaining 2 tablespoons butter. Cover, and bake 30 minutes.

5) Remove lid, increase heat to 400° and bake 15 minutes or until crisp and browned. Allow to rest 5 minutes before serving.

 Tip...Making stuffing in a skillet produces a bonus: one crust on top and one on the bottom.

mashed sweet potatoes with rosemary and orange

Prep: 10 min.   **Cook:** 5 min.   **Bake:** 30 min.   **Serves:** 8

SHOPPING LIST
4 (8-ounces each) sweet potatoes, peeled, diced
¼ cup canola oil
Salt and freshly ground black pepper to taste
½ cup unsalted butter
½ cup dark brown sugar
4 sprigs rosemary
Zest of 1 orange, grated (1 teaspoon)

1) Preheat oven to 425°.

2) Line rimmed baking sheet with parchment paper. Add sweet potatoes, and drizzle oil over top. Season with salt and pepper. Toss to evenly coat. Bake 30 minutes or until tender. Transfer to bowl. Set aside, and keep warm.

3) Melt butter and sugar in 10-inch skillet over medium-low heat. Add rosemary. Cook 5 minutes or until melted together. Remove and discard rosemary. Fold in zest.

4) Rewarm butter mixture over medium heat, and pour over sweet potatoes. Mash together using the back of a fork. Season to taste. Serve in serving bowl.

A word from Bob...

Adding fresh herbs near the end of cook time will elevate the flavor of most vegetables. Rosemary and potatoes are especially well suited for each other.

Tip...Extra rosemary sprigs along the sides of the serving bowl make a pretty garnish.

red potatoes and green beans with dijon vinaigrette

Prep: 10 min. **Cook:** 16 min. **Serves:** 8–12

SHOPPING LIST

½ pound fresh green beans, trimmed and cut into 1½-inch pieces
3 pounds small red-skinned potatoes, unpeeled, halved
2 tablespoons white wine vinegar
1½ tablespoons Dijon mustard
½ teaspoon ground black pepper
1 teaspoon dill
½ cup extra virgin olive oil

1) Cook beans in large saucepan of boiling water 4 minutes or until just tender. Drain. Cool under running cold water. Drain, and pat dry with paper towels.

2) Cook potatoes in large pot of boiling water about 12 minutes or until just tender. Drain. Transfer to large bowl.

3) Whisk vinegar, mustard, pepper, and dill in small bowl. Gradually whisk in oil. Pour over potatoes, and gently toss to coat without breaking potatoes. Cool completely. Mix in green beans. Gently toss to combine. Season with salt to taste. Serve cold or at room temperature.

 Tip...Try hot smoked paprika in place of the cayenne pepper. This dish can be made a day ahead of serving.

sweet onion casserole

Prep: 30 min.   **Cook:** 30 min.   **Serves:** 8–10

SHOPPING LIST
1 stick butter, divided
4 large Vidalia onions (about 4 pounds), peeled, halved and sliced into ¼-inch slices
24 classic round snack crackers, crumbled, divided
½ cup grated Pecorino Romano cheese, divided
2 tablespoons chopped parsley, divided

1) Preheat oven to 350°.

2) Melt butter in large oven-proof skillet. Sauté sliced onions about 10 minutes, until tender and slightly golden.

3) Layer half the onions into a 3-quart baking dish with half the crushed crackers and half the cheese. Repeat layers. Top with parsley.

4) Bake uncovered for 30 minutes or until golden brown and bubbly.

A word from Bob...

You can do this in the same oven-proof skillet by removing half the sautéed onions, layer half the crackers and cheese, return onions, layer remainder of crackers and cheese...Voila!
All in one skillet!

Tip...Put crackers into sandwich-size zip-lock bag, and crush with fingers. Add ¼ cup cheese. Shake to combine. Repeat in second zip-lock bag with remaining 12 crackers and ¼ cup cheese. Your portions are neatly divided and ready to use!

pecorino skillet-baked risotto with wild mushrooms

Prep: 8 min. **Cook:** 12 min. **Bake:** 40 min. **Serves:** 8

SHOPPING LIST

4 tablespoons unsalted butter, divided
1 tablespoon canola oil
5 ounces sliced shiitake mushrooms
Salt and freshly ground pepper to taste
1 large shallot, minced (2 tablespoons)
2 garlic cloves, minced
½ cup white wine
1 cup Arborio rice
2 tablespoons chicken or mushroom concentrate
3 cups water
½ cup shredded Pecorino Romano cheese
2 tablespoons chopped fresh tarragon

1) Preheat oven to 350°.

2) Melt 2 tablespoons butter and oil in 3-quart sauté pan over medium heat. Add mushrooms, season with salt and pepper and sauté 6 minutes, until tender.

3) Add shallot and garlic. Sauté 1 minute, until tender and fragrant. Add wine, and reduce by half, about 1 minute. Stir in rice to coat. Toast for 1 minute.

4) Combine chicken concentrate and water. Add to rice. Season with salt and pepper. Stir in cheese. Cover, and place in the oven 30 minutes. Uncover, and continue baking 8–10 minutes, until liquid is almost absorbed. Remove from oven. Fold in remaining 2 tablespoons butter until melted.

5) Divide among 4 pasta bowls, and garnish with tarragon.

 Tip...Arborio rice is an Italian short-grain rice which, when cooked, has rounded grains that are firm, creamy and chewy, perfect for risotto.

roasted asparagus with brown butter and lemon

Prep: 3 min. **Cook:** 5 min. **Bake:** 17 min. **Serves:** 4

SHOPPING LIST

1 bunch asparagus, dried and trimmed
1 tablespoon olive oil
Zest and juice (2 tablespoons) of 1 lemon
Salt and freshly ground black pepper to taste
3 tablespoons unsalted butter

1) Preheat oven to 400°.

2) Place asparagus on a rimmed baking sheet, drizzle oil and lemon juice over the top and season with salt and pepper. Toss to evenly coat. Bake 15–17 minutes, until tender, turning halfway through bake time.

3) Melt butter in 8-inch skillet over medium heat. Cook 3–4 minutes, swirling pan periodically, until milk solids become light brown and smell nutty. Remove from heat. Set aside.

4) Place asparagus on a serving plate. Drizzle butter over the top, and garnish with zest.

 Tip...Whisk ¼ teaspoon chicken concentrate into butter for an extra boost of flavor.

three bean bake with bacon

Prep: 25 min.   **Cook:** 60 min.   **Serves:** 6

SHOPPING LIST

6 slices, thick-cut, hardwood-smoked bacon, chopped before cooking to ½-inch pieces
1 large Vidalia onion, chopped (about 2 cups)
⅔ cup chopped green bell pepper
⅔ cup chopped red bell pepper
6 garlic cloves, pressed
1 (8-ounce) can tomato sauce
½ cup packed brown sugar
1 tablespoon cider vinegar
1 tablespoon Dijon mustard
1 teaspoon smoked paprika
½ teaspoon salt
¼ teaspoon ground black pepper
¼ teaspoon ground cayenne pepper
1 (15-ounce) can black beans, rinsed and drained
1 (15-ounce) can garbanzo beans, rinsed and drained
1 (15-ounce) can Great Northern beans, rinsed and drained

1) Preheat oven to 325°.

2) Heat oven-proof 12-inch nonstick skillet over medium-high heat. Add bacon to pan, and sauté for 5 minutes or until crisp. Transfer bacon from pan with a slotted spoon onto paper towels to drain. Reserve 1½ tablespoons of drippings in pan. Add onion, bell peppers, and garlic. Sauté for 6 minutes or until tender.

3) Whisk tomato sauce, sugar, vinegar, mustard, paprika, salt and ground peppers in large bowl. Stir into onion mixture along with beans.

4) Sprinkle with reserved bacon. Cover, and bake 30 minutes. Uncover, and bake an additional 30 minutes. Stir before serving.

eggplant tomato skillet gratin with mozzarella

Prep: 8 min. **Cook:** 10 min. **Bake:** 30 min. **Serves:** 6

SHOPPING LIST

3 tablespoons canola oil
1 eggplant, diced (5 cups)
1 onion, diced (1 cup)
1½ tablespoons chopped thyme leaves
Salt and freshly ground black pepper
3 garlic cloves, minced
2 tablespoons tomato paste
1 (15-ounce) can diced tomatoes
1¼ cups shredded mozzarella cheese
1 cup crushed garlic croutons

1) Preheat oven to 350°.

2) Place canola oil in 3-quart nonstick skillet over medium-high heat. When oil is heated, add eggplant, onion and thyme. Season with salt and pepper. Sauté 7–8 minutes or until tender.

3) Stir in garlic, and sauté 30–60 seconds, until fragrant. Stir in tomato paste, and sauté 30–60 seconds or until caramelized and well combined.

4) Stir in tomatoes, and season with salt and pepper. Cook 1 minute to warm through. Remove from heat. Sprinkle mozzarella on top. Bake 25–30 minutes, until liquid is almost absorbed and vegetables are moist.

5) Remove from oven, and top with croutons. Rest 5 minutes.

 Tip…To prepare croutons, place in a large zip-lock storage bag, push out the air, zip closed, and gently crush using the flat side of a mallet.

dijon glazed carrots

Prep: 10 min.   **Cook:** 10 min.
Serves: 4

SHOPPING LIST
1 (1-pound) package baby carrots
½ cup water
1 tablespoon butter
2 tablespoons brown sugar
¼ cup orange juice
1 tablespoon Dijon mustard
¼ teaspoon ground ginger
¼ teaspoon white pepper

1) Add carrots and water to 2½-quart saucepan, and bring to a boil. Reduce heat, and cook covered for 10 minutes or until tender. Drain. Transfer carrots to a serving dish, and keep warm.

2) Melt butter in same pan. Stir in sugar, juice, mustard, ginger, and pepper. Cook over medium heat until sugar is dissolved, stirring often. Pour sauce over carrots, and toss gently to coat.

Tip...Garnish with orange zest and chopped fresh parsley.

greek rice bake

Prep: 20 min.   **Cook:** 40 min.
Serves: 6–8

SHOPPING LIST
6 tablespoons butter
2 cups long-grain white rice
5 cups chicken broth
2 tablespoons lemon juice
¼ cup finely chopped red onion
1 teaspoon chopped fresh oregano
¼ teaspoon salt
⅛ teaspoon freshly ground black pepper
½ cup crumbled feta cheese

1) Preheat oven to 375°.

2) Melt butter in large oven-proof skillet. Add dry rice, and stir well to coat all rice grains with butter. Cook about 5 minutes over medium-high heat, stirring often, until rice is cream-colored. Do not brown.

3) Add broth, covering rice. Stir in lemon juice, onion, oregano, salt, and pepper. Rice will sink to bottom of pan.

4) Place skillet in oven, and bake uncovered 25 minutes. Remove from oven, and stir. Cover, and bake 10–15 more minutes, until liquid has absorbed.

5) Remove from oven, and let rest 2 minutes, unstirred. Sprinkle with feta, and serve.

Tip...Substitute ½ teaspoon dried oregano for fresh.

cauliflower with smoked paprika

Prep: 5 min.   **Cook:** 30 min   **Serves:** 4–6

SHOPPING LIST
1 head cauliflower
1 teaspoon smoked paprika
1 teaspoon salt
½ teaspoon black pepper
½ teaspoon red pepper flakes (optional)
2–4 tablespoons extra virgin olive oil

1) Preheat oven to 425°.

2) Remove cauliflower stem and leaves. Break head into smaller florets. Combine paprika, salt, pepper, red pepper flakes and oil in gallon-size zip-lock bag. Add cauliflower. Seal bag, squeezing out most air. Manipulate bag to combine ingredients, and coat cauliflower.

3) Transfer cauliflower to cookie sheet. Spread in single layer. Roast about 20 minutes. Turn cauliflower flower sides down, and roast 10 more minutes or until tender and beginning to brown.

 Tip...Change up the expectations by serving this cauliflower, cooked and cooled, with your favorite dip. Ranch is good!

spaghetti squash with pesto

Prep: 15 min. **Cook:** 30 min. **Serves:** 6

SHOPPING LIST
1 (2- to 3-pound) spaghetti squash
½ cup pine nuts
1 cup prepared pesto
Salt and freshly ground black pepper to taste
4 plum tomatoes, diced (about 1 cup), divided
Freshly grated Pecorino Romano cheese

1) Boil whole spaghetti squash in water to cover in Dutch oven about 30 minutes or until tender when pierced with knife.

2) Toast pine nuts over medium-low heat in small skillet. Shake skillet frequently to ensure even browning. Set aside when golden and fragrant. Heat pesto in small saucepan. Set aside. Keep warm.

3) Drain squash, and place on cutting board until cool to touch. Cut in half lengthwise. Using large spoon, remove seeds and strings in center of squash, and discard.

4) Scrape flesh of squash away from skin with a fork, and transfer back to Dutch oven. Season with salt and pepper to taste. Toss with tomatoes, reserving about 2 tablespoonfuls of tomatoes for garnish.

5) Put ½ cup squash on plate, and top with 1 tablespoon pesto. Sprinkle some tomatoes on top of pesto, and top with Pecorino Romano cheese to taste and pine nuts.

 Tip...Using two forks to toss squash and tomatoes works well to separate strands. Substitute well-drained canned diced tomatoes or chopped fresh grape tomatoes for fresh plum tomatoes.

savory corn pudding with salsa

Prep: 10 min. **Cook:** 50 min. **Serves:** 8

SHOPPING LIST
½ cup stone-ground cornmeal
1½ teaspoons baking powder
1 tablespoon sugar
½ teaspoon salt
3 eggs
¾ cup milk
2 tablespoons butter, melted
1 (14¾-ounce) can cream-style corn
2 cups frozen corn, thawed
½ cup medium salsa
1 tablespoon chopped cilantro
½ cup shredded Cheddar cheese

1) Preheat oven to 350°. Spray a 2-quart baking dish with nonstick cooking spray.

2) Combine cornmeal, baking powder, sugar and salt in a large bowl. Whisk together eggs, milk and butter in a smaller bowl. Whisk egg mixture with cornmeal mixture. Stir in corn, salsa and cilantro.

3) Pour into prepared baking dish. Bake 30 minutes, until top is starting to firm. Remove from oven, and increase temperature to 375°. Sprinkle Cheddar cheese over top. Return to oven, and bake 10 more minutes or until cheese turns golden. Let cool 10 minutes before serving.

Tip...Control the "heat" of this dish by using spicier or milder salsas.

apricot ginger chicken...p88

main dishes

Main dishes are what we seek—a dish that will have more than one meal component in it, tastes good, has a relatively easy and quick prep time, and will have our family begging to have this dish again soon! We have revisited some of the classics in this chapter, cooked in ways that preserve the flavor we love but with little "fussing" to make it come together.

The Italian Beef Stew is for those cozy days of winter, when we don't mind smelling the stew simmer for over an hour. This one is with farro, a food product from wheat that is catching on as an unusual yet delicious treat, cooked in flavorful liquid for a while. The Blue Cheese Burgers with Caramelized Onions are all dressed up for company, but are down home enough in taste to have on Wednesdays. Lemon Chicken Piccata cooks in only 16 minutes, but the joy of eating it will last for the whole week.

Capture some new tastes—like Baked Tandoori Chicken or Apricot Ginger Chicken, and be inspired by some fabulous new recipes.

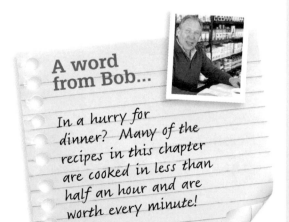

A word from Bob...

In a hurry for dinner? Many of the recipes in this chapter are cooked in less than half an hour and are worth every minute!

apricot ginger chicken

Prep: 10 min.   **Cook:** 25 min.
Serves: 4-6

SHOPPING LIST
1 tablespoon olive oil
6 bone-in chicken thighs
1 teaspoon salt
½ teaspoon freshly ground black pepper
1 tablespoon chopped onion
1 tablespoon minced fresh ginger
1 garlic clove, minced
½ cup apricot preserves
1 cup water
2 teaspoons chicken concentrate
1 tablespoon sliced green onions

1) Heat olive oil in 10-inch skillet. Season chicken with salt and pepper.   Brown chicken in batches over medium-high heat. Transfer to serving plate. Drain, reserving 1 tablespoon drippings in skillet.

2) Add onion, ginger and garlic to skillet. Cook over medium heat, until onion is tender.

3) Stir in apricot preserves, water and chicken concentrate. Bring to a boil. Return chicken to skillet. Reduce heat to low. Cook covered 15 minutes or until chicken is done. Sprinkle with green onions before serving.

chicken with mushrooms and wine

Prep: 10 min. **Cook:** 25 min. **Serves:** 4

SHOPPING LIST

1 tablespoon olive oil
4 boneless, skinless chicken breasts (about 1¼ pounds)
1 teaspoon salt
½ teaspoon freshly ground black pepper
2 tablespoons chopped onion
¼ pound sliced mushrooms
⅔ cup white wine
¼ cup heavy cream or half-and-half
Chopped parsley

1) Heat olive oil in a 10-inch skillet. Season chicken with salt and pepper. Brown chicken in batches over medium high heat. Transfer to serving plate.

2) Stir in onion and mushrooms. Cook over medium heat until vegetables are tender. Stir in wine to deglaze pan. Bring to a boil. Return chicken to skillet, and reduce heat to low. Cook covered for 15 minutes or until chicken is done.

3) Transfer chicken to serving plate. Stir cream into skillet, and cook until slightly reduced. Pour over chicken, and sprinkle with parsley.

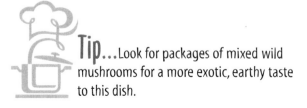

Tip...Look for packages of mixed wild mushrooms for a more exotic, earthy taste to this dish.

chicken with dumplings

Prep: 20 min. **Cook:** 40 min. **Serves:** 6

SHOPPING LIST
1 cup all-purpose flour
1 teaspoon salt
½ teaspoon ground pepper
6 bone-in skinless chicken thighs
2 tablespoons vegetable oil
1 medium onion, sliced (½ cup)
1 garlic clove, minced
2 tablespoons chicken concentrate
4 cups water
1 (12-ounce) package frozen mixed vegetables
1 cup baking mix
⅓ cup milk
2 teaspoons poultry seasoning

1) Combine flour, salt, and pepper in a plastic bag. Add chicken, and shake to coat.

2) Heat vegetable oil in Dutch oven over medium-high heat. Brown chicken, and transfer to serving dish. Lower heat to medium low, and cook onion and garlic until onion is tender.

3) Combine chicken concentrate and water. Add to Dutch oven. Return chicken to Dutch oven, stir in vegetables and bring to a boil. Reduce heat to low, and cook covered for 15 minutes.

4) Combine baking mix, milk and poultry seasoning in medium bowl. Uncover stew, and drop dough by tablespoons into boiling mixture. Cook uncovered 5 minutes. Cover, and cook 5 more minutes or until dumplings are firm.

chicken paprika with noodles

Prep: 5 min.   **Cook:** 25 min.   **Serves:** 4

SHOPPING LIST
½ cup all-purpose flour
¼ teaspoon ground red pepper
4 boneless, skinless chicken breasts
2 tablespoons vegetable oil
1 medium onion, chopped (1/2 cup)
1 garlic clove, minced
1 (10¾-ounce) can condensed cream of chicken soup
2 teaspoons paprika
1 (8-ounce) container sour cream
Hot cooked noodles

1)   Combine flour and red pepper on a plate. Coat chicken with flour mixture.

2)   Heat vegetable oil in 10-inch skillet. Brown chicken in batches over medium-high heat. Transfer to serving plate.

3)   Add onion and garlic to skillet. Cook until vegetables are tender. Stir in soup and paprika. Bring to a boil. Return chicken to skillet, and reduce heat to low. Cook covered for 15 minutes or until chicken is done.

4)   Stir in sour cream. Serve over noodles.

A word from Bob...

Condensed soup is a time-tested shortcut to a creamy sauce. Adding spices, herbs or a dash or two of lemon juice adds freshness to the finished sauce.

chicken parmesan burgers

Prep: 15 min.　**Cook:** 15 min.　**Serves:** 4

SHOPPING LIST

1 pound ground chicken
1 tablespoon chicken concentrate
¼ cup finely chopped fresh basil leaves
½ cup whole-grain plain bread crumbs
¼ cup shredded Parmesan cheese
1 tablespoon olive oil
1 cup tomato sauce
8 ounces fresh mozzarella cheese, cut into 8 slices
4 soft Italian-style hoagie rolls, split
Basil leaves for garnish

1) Preheat oven to 350°.

2) Combine chicken, concentrate, chopped basil, bread crumbs and Parmesan. Form into log-shaped patties (2x6 inches).

3) Heat olive oil in 10-inch nonstick skillet, and cook patties 8 minutes or until done, turning once.

4) Arrange Italian hoagie rolls on cookie sheet, and top each with a chicken patty. Drizzle 2 tablespoons tomato sauce onto each, then top with mozzarella. Bake 10 minutes or until cheese is melted and rolls are toasted. Garnish each with additional basil leaves.

 Tip...Save time by purchasing prepared chicken patties. Coat each in plain dry bread crumbs, and cook as described. Arrange on round Italian rolls, and continue as directed.

lemon chicken piccata

Prep: 10 min.   **Cook:** 16 min.   **Serves:** 4

SHOPPING LIST

1 pound boneless, skinless chicken breast halves, cut into 2½ inch pieces, pounded thin
Black pepper to taste
4 tablespoons all-purpose flour, divided
5 tablespoons unsalted butter, divided
2 tablespoons olive oil, divided
¼ cup finely chopped sweet onion
⅓ cup lemon juice
2 cups water
1 tablespoon chicken concentrate
2 tablespoons small capers
1 teaspoon finely grated lemon peel

1) Season chicken, if desired, with black pepper. Coat chicken in 3 tablespoons flour, reserving 1 tablespoon.

2) Melt 2 tablespoons butter with 1 tablespoon olive oil in deep 10-inch nonstick skillet over medium heat, and brown half the chicken for 4 minutes, turning once. Repeat with remaining chicken, 2 tablespoons butter and 1 tablespoon olive oil. Set aside.

3) Into same skillet, add onion, and cook 3 minutes or until starting to brown, stirring frequently. Sprinkle with remaining 1 tablespoon flour, and cook 1 minute. Stir in lemon juice, water and chicken concentrate, and bring to a boil. Reduce heat to low. Add chicken, capers, lemon peel and remaining 1 tablespoon butter to skillet. Simmer 4 minutes or until chicken is tender and cooked through. Garnish, if desired, with lemon slices.

Tip...Save time by purchasing thin-sliced chicken breasts. Serve this decadent chicken dish with crusty French bread to dip, and savor all the sauce!

baked tandoori chicken

Prep: 10 min.   **Cook:** 60 min.   **Serves:** 6

SHOPPING LIST
1½ pounds skinless boneless chicken thighs
1 teaspoon chili powder
½ teaspoon salt
1 (6-ounce) container plain yogurt
Juice of 1 lemon
1 teaspoon ground cumin
1 teaspoon ground coriander
1 teaspoon ground ginger
1 teaspoon garlic powder
2 tablespoons olive oil
2 tablespoons melted butter

1) Score chicken with sharp knife. Rub chicken with chili powder and salt.

2) Combine yogurt with lemon juice, cumin, coriander, ginger, garlic powder and oil in large bowl. Add chicken, turning to coat. Marinate covered in refrigerator up to 2 hours.

3) Preheat oven to 375°.

4) Place rack in 5-quart nonstick saucepot. Arrange chicken on rack. Bake, brushing with butter occasionally, 1 hour or until chicken is dark golden brown and cooked though. Serve with hot cooked rice, couscous or quinoa, and garnish with lemons.

 **Tip**...Substitute 4 teaspoons of your favorite garam masala blend. Line bottom and sides of saucepot with aluminum foil for quick cleanup.

chicken and broccoli with creamy cheese sauce

Prep: 15 min.   **Cook:** 10 min.   **Serves:** 6

SHOPPING LIST

¼ cup all-purpose flour
2 cups water
1 tablespoon chicken concentrate
1 cup milk
1½ cups shredded Cheddar cheese
2 ounces cream cheese
¾ teaspoon salt
¼ teaspoon freshly ground black pepper
4 cups bite-size broccoli florets, blanched
1 pound penne pasta, cooked according to package directions
1 rotisserie chicken, shredded

1) Melt 4 tablespoons butter in 10-inch-deep nonstick skillet over medium hear. Add flour and cook 4 minutes or until golden brown, stirring constantly. Gradually whisk in water, and bring to a boil. Stir in concentrate, milk, cheeses, salt and pepper. Reduce heat to low, and simmer, stirring occasionally, 4 minutes or until cheese is melted and sauce is thickened.

2) Stir in broccoli, and heat through. Toss sauce with pasta, and garnish with chicken.

Tip...The chicken concentrate really boosts the flavor of the cheese sauce with its depth of flavor.

turkey reuben panini

Prep: 5 min. **Cook:** 10 min. **Serves:** 4

SHOPPING LIST
8 teaspoons butter, softened
8 slices rye or rye pumpernickel swirl bread
½ cup prepared Thousand Island or Russian salad dressing
4 ounces thinly sliced deli Swiss cheese
8 ounces thinly sliced deli roast turkey or chicken
1 (8-ounce) can sauerkraut, rinsed and drained well

1) Heat grill pan or a cast-iron skillet over medium heat.

2) Spread butter on 1 side of each bread slice. Turn bread slices over, and spread each with 2 tablespoons salad dressing. Top four slices bread each with 1 slice turkey, 2 heaping tablespoons sauerkraut and another slice cheese. Top with remaining 4 slices bread, buttered side up.

3) Place each sandwich on the grill pan, and cook 3–4 minutes per side, pressing down occasionally with a spatula. Cut each sandwich in half, and serve immediately.

A word from Bob...

A shortcut to making paninis is to have the ingredients all assembled, bread buttered, while the pan heats. Nonstick is the way to go!

Tip...For a flavor and texture twist, substitute 4 ounces thinly sliced deli sharp Cheddar cheese for Swiss cheese. Substitute 8 ounces of your favorite prepared coleslaw, well drained, for sauerkraut.

korean barbecue chicken tacos

Prep: 20 min. **Marinate:** 2–4 hours **Cook:** 15 min. **Serves:** 6

SHOPPING LIST

4 boneless, skinless chicken breasts
4 tablespoons rice wine vinegar, divided
6 tablespoons honey, divided
2 tablespoons chili oil
2 tablespoons tamari or soy sauce
2 tablespoons lime juice
2 tablespoons vegetable oil
¼ teaspoon red pepper flakes
2 cups shredded romaine lettuce
1 cup shredded Napa cabbage
1 red bell pepper, thinly sliced
1 bunch green onions, white and light green parts trimmed, sliced
½ cup very thinly sliced sweet onion
¼ cup cilantro leaves
6 burrito-size flour tortillas, warmed

1) Marinate chicken 2–4 hours in 2 tablespoons vinegar, 2 tablespoons honey and chili oil.

2) Blend remaining 2 tablespoons vinegar, remaining 2 tablespoons honey, tamari, lime juice, vegetable oil and pepper flakes for vinaigrette.

3) Cook chicken in 10-inch nonstick skillet over medium-high heat, 10 minutes or until dark golden brown, turning once. Remove skillet from heat; let stand covered 5 minutes. Thinly slice chicken and combine with any juices from the skillet.

4) Toss lettuce, cabbage, bell pepper, onion and cilantro with half the vinaigrette in large bowl. Evenly arrange lettuce mixture on tortillas, and top with chicken. Evenly drizzle chicken with remaining vinaigrette.

Tip...Save time by purchasing prewashed, bagged Asian salad greens. Substitute them for lettuce and cabbage. This makes a terrific main-dish salad without the tortillas.

tuna noodle casserole

Prep: 5 min.   **Cook:** 30 min.   **Serves:** 4

SHOPPING LIST

2 cups medium egg noodles
1 (12-ounce) package frozen mixed vegetables (about 2 ¼ cups)
2 (5-ounce) cans tuna, drained
1 (10¾-ounce) can condensed cream of mushroom soup
1 cup milk
4 tablespoons grated Parmesan cheese, divided
½ teaspoon garlic powder
¼ teaspoon freshly ground black pepper
3 tablespoons panko bread crumbs
1 tablespoon butter, melted

1) Preheat oven to 350°. Fill 2½-quart saucepan ⅔ full of water. Heat water to a boil. Add noodles, and cook for 5 minutes. Drain, and set aside.

2) Combine vegetables, tuna, soup, reserved noodles, milk, 3 tablespoons cheese, garlic powder and pepper in the skillet. Mix well. Place skillet in oven. Bake 20 minutes or until mixture is hot and bubbling.

3) Combine bread crumbs, butter and remaining 1 tablespoon cheese in small bowl.

4) Stir tuna mixture. Sprinkle with bread crumb mixture. Bake 10 more minutes or until bread crumbs are lightly golden brown.

 Tip...To brown bread crumb topping faster, preheat broiler and broil mixture about 6 inches from heat, 3–4 minutes or until golden brown. Substitute 1 (2.8-ounce) container French fried onions for bread crumb mixture. Bake 3–4 minutes or until onions are golden brown.

italian beef stew with farro

Prep: 15 min.   **Cook:** 2 hours   **Serves:** 6

SHOPPING LIST

3 tablespoons beef of mushroom concentrate, divided
4 cups water
½ ounce dried porcini mushrooms
2 tablespoons olive oil
2 pounds beef chuck, cut into 2-inch pieces
1 teaspoon salt
½ teaspoon ground pepper
1 large onion, chopped (1 cup)
2 slices thick-cut bacon or pancetta
2 carrots, thinly sliced (1 cup)
4 whole cloves
2 sprigs fresh rosemary
2 tablespoons tomato paste
2 bay leaves
2 cups red wine
1 (14-ounce) can plum tomatoes
1 cup farro

1) Heat beef concentrate and water in saucepan over medium heat just until boiling. Remove from heat. Add porcini mushrooms, and soak for 30 minutes. Strain, and reserve soaking liquid.

2) Heat 2 tablespoons olive oil in Dutch oven over medium-high heat.   Brown beef in batches. Transfer to serving plate. Season with salt and pepper.

3) Add onion and bacon to Dutch oven, and cook until onion is tender. Add carrots, cloves, rosemary, tomato paste and bay leaves. Stir in reserved liquid, wine, and tomatoes. Return beef to pot. Bring to a boil. Cover, reduce heat to low and cook for 1½ hours. Stir in farro, and cook for 40 minutes or until farro is tender. Remove bay leaves before serving.

Tip...Farro will remind you of barley—really good.

polenta bolognese

Prep: 10 min. **Cook:** 45 min. **Serves:** 8

SHOPPING LIST
Sauce:
¼ cup extra virgin olive oil
1 medium onion, coarsely chopped (about 1 cup)
2 garlic cloves, peeled, coarsely chopped
1 large celery stalk, coarsely chopped (½ cup)
1 large carrot, coarsely chopped (½ cup)
1 pound ground beef
1 (28-ounce) can crushed tomatoes
Freshly grated Pecorino Romano cheese
1 tablespoon chopped Italian flat-leaf parsley or basil for garnish

Polenta:
6 cups water
½ teaspoon salt
1¾ cups dry polenta or yellow cornmeal
3 tablespoons butter

Tip...When company's coming, jazz up this dish by adding 1 cup halved cherry tomatoes and thinly sliced basil leaves to the sauce when returning steaks to the skillet. In a pinch for time, substitute 16 ounces of your favorite pasta sauce. Cook the steaks, simmer the prepared sauce and add back the steaks.

Sauce:
1) Heat oil over medium-high heat in a large skillet. Add onion and garlic, and heat until onion becomes very soft, about 8 minutes. Add celery and carrot, and sauté for 5 minutes.

2) Raise heat to high, and add ground beef, helping it to break apart; mix with vegetables. Cook until meat is no longer pink, about 10 minutes.

3) Add tomatoes; stir together. Reduce heat to medium low. Cook about 30 minutes.

4) While sauce is cooking, prepare polenta.

Polenta:
1) Boil 6 cups water in large saucepan. Stir in salt. Gradually whisk in polenta or cornmeal, and reduce heat to low. Cook 10–15 minutes, until thickened, stirring frequently. Turn off heat, and stir in butter until melted and well distributed.

2) Spray 8x8-inch pan with nonstick cooking spray. Pour mixture in pan, and spread evenly. Let cool 10 minutes or until firm. Invert onto cutting surface.

3) Cut into 4 squares. Cut each square diagonally into 2 triangles. Place a triangle on each serving plate. Top each with ½ cup sauce. Sprinkle with cheese to taste. Garnish with parsley or basil leaf.

blue cheese burgers with caramelized onions

Prep: 15 min. **Cook:** 15 min.
Serves: 4

SHOPPING LIST

1 large sweet onion, thinly sliced
1 pound ground beef
½ cup crumbled blue cheese
1 tablespoon Worcestershire sauce
1 garlic clove, finely chopped
¼ teaspoon sea salt
⅛ teaspoon freshly ground black pepper
4 burger-sized ciabatta rolls, split
  and toasted
8 large basil leaves

1) Melt 1 tablespoon butter in 10-inch nonstick skillet over low heat. Cook onion 20 minutes or until dark golden brown, stirring occasionally. Keep warm.

2) Combine beef, cheese, sauce, garlic, salt, and pepper. Form into 4 patties. Grill or broil patties until cooked to desired doneness. Evenly arrange on rolls, and top generously with warm onions and basil leaves. Serve, if desired, with your favorite flavored mayonnaise.

steak pizziaola over spaghetti

Prep: 10 min. **Cook:** 15 min. **Serves:** 4–6

SHOPPING LIST

4–6 thin-sliced boneless choice beef chuck
  steaks (about 1 pound)
¾ teaspoon salt, divided
¾ teaspoon black pepper, divided
1½ teaspoons dried oregano, divided
1 tablespoon plus 1 teaspoon olive oil, divided
½ cup thinly sliced onion
2 garlic cloves, finely chopped
1 tablespoon tomato paste
1 (15-ounce) can tomato sauce
1 pound spaghetti, cooked according to package directions, reserving ¼ cup pasta water
¼ cup shredded Parmesan cheese

1) Season each steak with ¼ teaspoon salt, black pepper and oregano.

2) Heat 1 tablespoon olive oil in deep 10-inch nonstick skillet, and cook steaks, turning once, 6 minutes or until desired doneness; transfer to plate to reserve juices.

3) In same skillet, heat 1 teaspoon olive oil and cook onion 4 minutes or until tender, stirring occasionally. Add garlic, and cook 30 seconds or until fragrant. Stir in tomato paste, and cook 1 minute, stirring constantly. Stir in tomato sauce, salt, pepper and reserved pasta water; bring to a boil. Reduce heat, and simmer 10 minutes.

4) Return steaks and any juices to skillet. Simmer just until steaks are reheated. Serve steaks over spaghetti tossed with sauce. Sprinkle with cheese.

easy pasta puttanesca

Prep: 5 min. **Cook:** 25 min. **Serves:** 6

SHOPPING LIST
2 tablespoons olive oil
4 garlic cloves, minced
1 (10½-ounce) can condensed French onion soup
1 (14½-ounce) can diced fire-roasted tomatoes, undrained
⅓ cup pitted kalamata olives, halved
3 tablespoons capers, rinsed and drained
⅛ teaspoon crushed red bell pepper
2 teaspoons anchovy paste
1 pound spaghetti or linguine pasta
½ cup chopped fresh basil
½ cup fresh grated Parmesan cheese

1) Heat olive oil over medium heat in 9½-inch deep-sided skillet. Add garlic, and cook 1 minute or until fragrant, stirring constantly. Add soup, tomatoes and liquid, olives, capers, pepper and anchovy paste. Bring to a boil. Reduce heat to medium, and cook 10 minutes or until mixture is reduced to 2 cups.

2) Fill 5-quart saucepot ⅔ full of water. Heat water to a boil. Add spaghetti, and cook, following package directions, or until al dente. Drain spaghetti.

3) Toss hot cooked spaghetti with finished sauce. Top with basil and cheese.

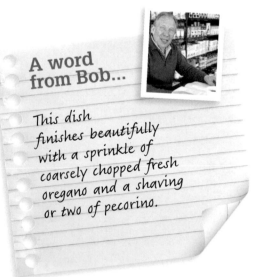

A word from Bob...

This dish finishes beautifully with a sprinkle of coarsely chopped fresh oregano and a shaving or two of pecorino.

Tip...Substitute 2 anchovy fillets, drained and chopped, for anchovy paste. Substitute your favorite whole-wheat spaghetti or linguine for regular pasta.

burgundy braised beef with onions and mushrooms

Prep: 20 min. **Cook:** 2 hours **Serves:** 6

SHOPPING LIST

4 ounces thick-cut bacon, cut into 1-inch pieces
2 pounds beef chuck, cut into 2-inch pieces
1 teaspoon salt
½ teaspoon ground pepper
1 large onion, chopped (1 cup)
4 garlic cloves, chopped
2 celery stalks, cut into 2-inch pieces
1 tablespoon tomato paste
5 sprigs thyme
2 bay leaves
1 cup water
2 teaspoons beef or mushroom concentrate
1 cup red wine
1 large carrot, cut into 1-inch pieces (about 1 cup)
2 cups mushrooms, quartered

1) Cook bacon in Dutch oven over medium-high heat until browned. Remove from Dutch oven; drain.

2) Season beef with salt and pepper. Brown beef in batches. Transfer to serving plate. Add onion, garlic and celery. Cook until tender. Stir in tomato paste, thyme and bay leaves. Return beef to pot. Stir in water, beef concentrate and wine.

3) Bring to a boil, then reduce heat to low. Cook covered for 1 ½ hours. Add carrot and mushrooms, and cook for 30 minutes or until beef and vegetables are tender. Remove bay leaf before serving.

pork tenderloin with dried cherry port sauce

Prep: 5 min. **Cook:** 10 min. **Serves:** 4

SHOPPING LIST
2 tablespoons butter, divided
1 pork tenderloin, cut into ¾-inch-thick slices (about 1 pound)
Salt and freshly ground black pepper to taste
1 large shallot, finely minced (about ¼ cup)
2 garlic cloves, minced
2 tablespoons tawny port
2 cups water
1 tablespoon chicken concentrate, divided
1 tablespoon cornstarch
⅓ cup dried cherries (about 2 ounces)
1 tablespoon chopped fresh rosemary

1) Melt 1 tablespoon butter in 9½-inch deep-sided skillet over medium-high heat. Season pork with salt and pepper. Add pork, and cook until well browned on both sides. Transfer pork to serving dish.

2) Melt remaining 1 tablespoon butter in skillet. Add shallot and garlic, and cook about 3 minutes, until vegetables are tender-crisp. Carefully add port, and cook 1 minute.

3) In small bowl, combine water with chicken concentrate. Add 2 tablespoons of the broth to the cornstarch. Set aside.

4) Add remaining broth, cherries, and rosemary to skillet. Bring to a boil. Reduce heat to medium, and cook about 12 minutes, until reduced by half (about 1 cup). Stir reserved broth mixture, and add to skillet. Bring to a boil, stirring constantly until mixture thickens. Return pork to skillet, and heat through.

Tip... Substitute ⅓ cup dried cranberries for dried cherries and 1 tablespoon chopped fresh sage for the rosemary.

skillet pork with apples, onions and sauerkraut

Prep: 10 min.   **Cook:** 20 min.   **Serves:** 4

SHOPPING LIST
1 tablespoon canola oil
4 boneless pork chops, trimmed (1¼ pounds)
Salt and pepper to taste
2 large onions, sliced (about 2 cups)
2 tart cooking apples, cored and sliced (about 2 cups)
1 (15-ounce) can sauerkraut, rinsed and drained
¼ cup hot water
1 teaspoon chicken concentrate
2 tablespoons packed brown sugar
1 teaspoon Dijon mustard
1 teaspoon caraway seed

1) Heat canola oil in 9½-inch deep-sided skillet over medium-high heat. Season pork chops with salt and pepper. Add pork chops, and cook about 8 minutes, until browned on both sides. Transfer pork chops to serving plate.

2) Add onions and apples to skillet. Cook about 5 minutes until tender-crisp, stirring often. Transfer onions and apples to serving plate.

3) Add sauerkraut, water, chicken concentrate, sugar, mustard and caraway seed to skillet. Mix gently. Bring to a boil. Reduce heat to medium, and cook 5 minutes, stirring occasionally. Return onions and apples, and mix gently. Top mixture with pork chops. Cook covered 5 minutes or until pork chops are heated through.

4) Serve pork chops over sauerkraut mixture. Top with freshly cracked black pepper.

 **Tip**...Use Granny Smith apples and add ⅓ cup dried cranberries to sauerkraut mixture.

spiced apple puffed pancakes...p115

brunch

Brunch is undoubtedly the most fun meal for entertaining—no one has to arrive too early on a weekend day, there is plenty of evening left after the event, and usually everyone is in a sunny mood. Planning the menu is often the most time-consuming part, and we have done all that for you. The next step is to see what you can do ahead of time to keep the stress level manageable.

Our first recipe, Puffed Pancakes, opens the door to a dramatic offering for a romantic brunch for two. Pair it with our Sparkling White Sangria, and you can linger for hours.

For a larger crowd of eight, reach for our Spinach, Mushroom and Fontina Frittata and the Savory Sausage Breakfast Rolls. Both can be assembled and even prepared in advance, waiting for service with a fresh fruit salad.

Planning an elegant brunch for family or friends? Few main dishes will dazzle like the Easy Crabmeat Strudel or the Salmon Pockets. Add Spicy Bloody Mary with Shrimp Skewers, and you will have food memories to last a long time.

A word from Bob...

Let us help you plan brunch and other entertaining events! Here are some of your favorite recipes as well as some new, inviting variations!

puffed pancakes

Prep: 15 min. **Cook:** 25 min.
Serves: 4–6

SHOPPING LIST
2 tablespoons butter
3 eggs
¾ cup all-purpose flour
¾ cup milk, heated 20–30 seconds in
  microwave
1 tablespoon sugar
2 teaspoons pure vanilla extract
Pinch of salt
Confectioners' sugar for dusting

1) Preheat oven to 400°. Add butter
to nonstick 10-inch sauté pan, and
transfer to oven.

2) Combine eggs, flour, milk, sugar, vanilla and salt in blender. Process on
medium high until well mixed.

3) Remove pan from oven. Swirl
melted butter around the pan to coat
completely. Add egg mixture to pan,
and return to the oven.

4) Cook 20–25 minutes or until pancake
is puffed in the center and golden
brown along the edges. Remove the
entire pancake from the pan with
spatula. Cut into wedges, and serve
with desired filling.

Tip...Fresh or sautéed fruit is com-
monly used for the fillings, but you can
squeeze some fresh lemon juice, lemon
curd, whipped cream, any pie filling or
vanilla yogurt as a filling.

spiced apple puffed pancakes

spiced apple puffed pancakes

Prep: 15 min.   **Cook:** 25 min.   **Serves:** 4–6

SHOPPING LIST

Apple Topping:

1 tablespoon butter

2 Granny Smith apples, peeled, cored and sliced

2 tablespoons brown sugar

½ teaspoon ground cinnamon

Pancake:

3 eggs

¾ cup all-purpose flour

¾ cup milk, heated 20–30 seconds in microwave

1 tablespoon sugar

2 teaspoons pure vanilla extract

Pinch of salt

2 tablespoons butter

Confectioners' sugar for dusting

1) Preheat oven to 400°.

2) **Apple Topping:** Melt butter in 10-inch nonstick skillet over medium heat. Add apples, sugar and cinnamon, and cook 5 minutes or until apples are tender. Transfer to bowl, and keep warm. Wipe skillet clean.

3) **Pancake:** Combine eggs, flour, milk, sugar, vanilla and salt in blender. Process on medium high until well blended.

4) Add 2 tablespoons butter to nonstick 10-inch sauté pan, and transfer to oven. Heat until butter is melted.

5) Swirl melted butter around the pan to coat completely. Add egg mixture to pan, and return to the oven. Cook 20–25 minutes, until pancake is puffed in the center and golden brown along the edges. Remove the entire pancake from the pan with spatula. Serve with Apple Topping.

savory sausage breakfast rolls

Prep: 20 min. **Cook:** 20–25 min.
Serves: 8

SHOPPING LIST
1 pound bulk sausage
1 small onion, minced
1 teaspoon dried thyme
¼ teaspoon red pepper flakes
1 (11-ounce) package refrigerated
  pizza dough
½ cup grated Parmesan cheese

1) Cook sausage in tall skillet over
   medium heat until golden and
   crumbling. Add onion, thyme and
   pepper flakes. Cook 4–5 minutes
   or until onion is tender-crisp. Remove from heat, and cool.

2) On a lightly floured surface, roll
   dough to 14x12-inch rectangle.
   Distribute sausage evenly on
   dough, leaving 1-inch border all
   around. Sprinkle with Parmesan.
   Starting with the long side, roll
   dough jellyroll style. Pinch ends to
   seal.

3) Cut into 2-inch rolls, and place
   cut side down in the same skillet.
   Cook for 20–25 minutes or until
   rolls are golden brown. Serve with
   tomato sauce or scrambled eggs, if
   desired.

bread and butter pudding

Prep: 40 min. **Cook:** 35 min. **Serves:** 6

SHOPPING LIST
⅓ cup packed golden raisins
¼ cup brandy
12 slices cinnamon-swirl bread with raisins,
  toasted brown
3 tablespoons unsalted butter, room temperature
2 large eggs
2 large egg yolks
2 cups whole milk
1 cup heavy cream
1 tablespoon sugar
1 teaspoon vanilla extract
Confectioners' sugar for dusting

1) Adjust oven rack to center shelf, and preheat
   oven to 375°.

2) Place raisins in a small bowl, and pour brandy
   over them. Set aside.

3) On a clean work surface, lay out bread slices,
   and butter one side. Cut slices into triangles.
   Arrange bread buttered side down in 1½-quart
   baking dish, overlapping and layering. Drain
   raisins, and sprinkle on top of slices.

4) Whisk eggs, milk, cream, sugar and vanilla in
   a bowl. Pour mixture over bread. Rest for 15
   minutes to allow mixture to soak into bread.

5) Place baking dish on sheet pan. Bake 35 minutes or until set. Cool to room temperature,
   and dust with confectioners' sugar.

cheese blintz casserole with blueberries

Prep: 5 min.   **Cook:** 40 min.   **Serves:** 8

SHOPPING LIST
2 tablespoons butter, melted
3 cups sour cream
6 eggs
½ cup orange juice
½ cup sugar
1 teaspoon vanilla extract
½ teaspoon orange zest
2 (13-ounce) packages frozen cheese blintzes
1 pint blueberries
Cinnamon to taste

1) Place butter in 13x9-inch baking pan. Mix together sour cream, eggs, orange juice, sugar, vanilla extract and zest in medium bowl.

2) Arrange blintzes in pan, and coat with the melted butter. Sprinkle with blueberries.

3) Pour egg mixture over blintzes, and sprinkle with cinnamon. Bake for 40 minutes at 350°. Let stand 5 minutes before serving.

spinach, mushroom and fontina frittata

Prep: 20 min.   **Cook:** 25 min.   **Stand:** 20 min.   **Serves:** 8

SHOPPING LIST
2 tablespoons olive oil
2 cups sliced onions
8 ounces sliced mushrooms
1½ cups frozen chopped spinach, thawed and squeezed dry
8 eggs
1 cup milk
2 teaspoons mushroom or chicken concentrate
1 cup grated Italian fontina cheese
Salt and freshly ground black pepper to taste

1) Preheat oven to 375°.

2) Heat oil in tall nonstick skillet over medium heat. Stir in onion and mushrooms. Sauté 12–14 minutes or until golden brown and dry. Distribute spinach in even layer over mushrooms.

3) Whisk eggs, milk, mushroom concentrate and cheese in a bowl. Season mixture with salt and pepper. Pour egg mixture over onion mixture, and stir gently. Cook 3–4 minutes, until a firm bottom layer forms.

4) Place pan in oven, and cook 18–20 minutes or until mixture firms. Remove from oven and let stand 5 minutes. Turn frittata bottom side up onto cutting board. Let stand 15 minutes before cutting. Serve warm or at room temperature, cut into squares or wedges.

mediterranean omelet

Prep: 5 min.   **Cook:** 5 min.   **Serves:** 1

SHOPPING LIST
3 eggs
1 tablespoon water
1 tablespoon chopped chives
Salt and cracked black pepper to taste
1 tablespoon olive oil
½ cup coarsely chopped spinach leaves
¼ cup halved grape tomatoes
2 tablespoons crumbled feta cheese

1) Beat eggs, water, chives, salt and pepper in a small bowl.

2) Heat oil in 6-inch skillet over high heat. Drop a little egg into the hot oil. If it bubbles, add
    eggs to the skillet. Let cook a few seconds, then use fork or high-heat spatula to move egg
    mixture from sides to middle. Add spinach, and cook until eggs are set.

3) Reduce heat to medium. Add tomatoes and cheese to the lower third of the skillet. Cook
    lightly to heat ingredients (30–40 seconds). Fold egg mixture over to cover tomatoes and
    cheese, and roll omelet out of the pan. Serve with toasted bread.

A word from Bob...

If you really love Mediterranean foods, add some sliced or chopped kalamata olives to this terrific omelet.

zucchini and roasted pepper strata

Prep: 20 min.   **Cook:** 20-25 min.   **Serves:** 6

SHOPPING LIST
5 eggs
1 cup milk
1 cup grated Parmesan cheese
Salt and freshly ground black pepper to taste
6 cups cubed Italian bread
2 tablespoons olive oil
1 cup diced onion
2 cups shredded zucchini
1 cup diced roasted red peppers
6 cups cubed Italian bread

1) Prehcat oven to 350°.

2) Combine eggs, milk, cheese, salt and pepper in a bowl. Add bread, and let stand 20 minutes, stirring occasionally.

3) Heat olive oil in tall skillet over medium heat. Add onion, and cook 3–4 minutes or until tender-crisp. Add zucchini, and cook until dry. Add red peppers, and cook 1 minute.

4) Pour egg mixture over vegetables, and place in preheated oven. Bake for 20–25 minutes or until firm to the touch.

 Tip...Changing the vegetables and the cheese gives you endless variations. For example, try broccoli and Cheddar to replace zucchini and Parmesan.

ricotta and roasted vegetable pizza

Prep: 20 min. **Cook:** 30 min. **Serves:** 6–8

SHOPPING LIST

2 tablespoons olive oil
2 cups sliced sweet onion
2 teaspoons chopped garlic
2 cups diced zucchini
1 cup sliced red bell pepper
1 cup plum tomatoes, coarsely chopped
1 teaspoon oregano
Salt and cracked black pepper to taste
1 pound prepared pizza dough
½ cup grated Parmesan cheese
3 tablespoons chopped parsley
1 cup ricotta cheese

1) Preheat oven to 400°.

2) Heat oil in tall sauté pan. Add onion, and sauté 3–4 minutes or until tender-crisp. Add garlic, zucchini, bell pepper, tomatoes and oregano. Cook 5–6 minutes or until little liquid remains. Season vegetables with salt and pepper.

3) Roll dough on a lightly floured surface to create 12-inch circle. Carefully place dough over vegetables in pan, tucking in sides to create border. Place pan in oven, and bake 22–25 minutes or until crust is golden and firm. Remove pan from heat, and let stand 5 minutes before inverting onto platter or cutting board.

4) Sprinkle pizza with Parmesan cheese, parsley and ricotta. Cut into wedges, and serve with a mixed greens salad.

 Tip...Seasonal vegetables can be used such as asparagus and eggplant. Ground cooked sausage makes a flavorful addition.

easy crabmeat strudel

Prep: 30 min. **Cook:** 17 min. **Serves:** 6–8

SHOPPING LIST
1 stick unsalted butter, melted, divided
2 tablespoons minced shallots
3 green onions, white and pale green parts,
   trimmed and minced (¼ cup)
½ cup finely diced red bell pepper
2 (6-ounce) cans fancy lump crabmeat in water,
   drained, cartilage removed
2 tablespoons minced chives
2 tablespoons lemon juice
Salt and freshly ground black pepper to taste
10 sheets phyllo dough
¼ cup plain dry bread crumbs

1) Adjust oven rack to center shelf. Preheat oven to 400°. Cover sheet pan with parchment paper, and set aside.

2) Add 2 tablespoons melted butter to 10½-inch nonstick skillet. Cook shallots, green onions and red pepper over medium-high heat. Stir to combine, and sauté for 5 minutes or until vegetables are soft.

3) Shred crabmeat with a fork in a bowl. Add vegetable mixture, chives, lemon juice, salt and pepper.

4) Unfold 1 package phyllo dough. Brush 1 sheet with melted butter, and sprinkle with bread crumbs. Repeat process, placing second phyllo over first. Repeat until 5 sheets have been used.

5) Spoon half the crabmeat mixture on lower edge of phyllo dough, leaving a border of about 1 inch on each side. Roll up the strudel, tucking in the sides, and place seam-side down on parchment-lined sheet pan. Brush with butter on top and sides. Repeat process with remaining phyllo and crabmeat.

6) Score strudel diagonally into 1½-inch pieces, and bake for 12 minutes or until top is lightly golden brown. Slice, and serve.

salmon pockets

Prep: 25 min. **Cook:** 26 min. **Serves:** 4

SHOPPING LIST
2 tablespoons olive oil
2 tablespoons minced shallots
4 tablespoons lemon juice (1 lemon)
¼ cup sun-dried tomatoes, minced in food processor
   or chopped fine
1 tablespoon dried herbes de Provence
¼ cup dried plain bread crumbs
Salt and freshly ground black pepper to taste
½ (17.3-ounce) package puff pastry sheets
   (1 sheet), thawed
2 (12-ounce) skinless salmon fillets
1 large egg, beaten with 1 tablespoon water

Tip...Brown the salmon fillets on both sides for extra flavor.

1) Preheat oven to 400°.

2) Heat olive oil in a 10½-inch nonstick skillet over medium heat. Add shallots, and sauté about 5 minutes, until lightly colored.

3) Add juice, sun-dried tomatoes, herbs, bread crumbs, salt and pepper. Cook for 1 minute, stirring until incorporated. Transfer mixture to a bowl.

4) Lightly dust a clean work surface with flour. Open pastry, and roll sheet to measure 14x12 inches. Cut sheet in half horizontally.

5) Season salmon on both sides with salt and pepper. Spread half the tomato mixture down center of pastry. Place 1 salmon fillet on top of mixture. Brush edges of pastry with egg mixture, and pull up all 4 sides of pastry dough to enclose like a package. Brush with egg mixture.

6) Place pockets seam side down on a sheet pan lined with parchment paper. Brush top and sides with egg mixture.

7) Slash 3 vents on top with a sharp knife. Repeat process using remaining salmon, tomato mixture and pastry. Place pockets in oven, and bake for 20 minutes or until pastry is puffed and golden brown. Slice each salmon puff pastry in half, and serve.

apple sausage patties

Prep: 30 min. **Cook:** 25 min. **Serves:** 4

SHOPPING LIST

1 pound lean ground pork
1 medium garlic clove, minced (1 teaspoon)
1 teaspoon minced fresh thyme leaves
1 teaspoon minced fresh sage leaves
½ Granny Smith apple, peeled and grated (½ cup)
½ cup fresh bread crumbs
1 large egg yolk
1 tablespoon applesauce
Salt and freshly ground black pepper to taste
½ cup dry plain bread crumbs, spread on a plate
1 tablespoon butter
1 tablespoon canola oil
1 cup dry white wine
1 teaspoon chicken concentrate

1) Combine pork, garlic, thyme, sage, apple, fresh bread crumbs, egg yolk, applesauce, salt and pepper. Mix well with a fork.

2) Divide pork mixture into 4 round patties about 3 inches across and 1 inch thick. Dredge in dry bread crumbs, coating both sides well.

3) Heat butter and oil in 10-inch sauté pan over medium-high heat. Brown patties 5 minutes each side.

4) Add wine and chicken concentrate. Bring to a boil, and reduce heat to medium low. Cook covered 10 minutes.

5) Uncover pan, and turn patties over. Raise heat, and cook 5 more minutes or until sauce has reduced and thickened. Serve patties with sauce and buttered noodles, if desired.

Tip...For a non-alcoholic sauce, substitute apple juice for wine.

huevos rancheros

Prep: 25 min. **Cook:** 30 min. **Serves:** 4

SHOPPING LIST
5 tablespoons vegetable oil, divided
1 medium onion, chopped (1 cup)
2 large garlic cloves, minced (1 tablespoon)
1 (28-ounce) can chopped Italian tomatoes, undrained (3 cups)
2 jalapeño peppers, seeded and minced
1 teaspoon ground cumin
Salt and freshly ground black pepper to taste
4 green onions, white and pale green parts, trimmed and chopped (¼ cup)
2 tablespoons chopped cilantro
4 corn tortillas
8 large eggs

1) Heat 2 tablespoons oil in large nonstick sauté pan over medium heat. Add onion and garlic. Cook 10 minutes or until soft. Add tomatoes, peppers and cumin. Cook 5 minutes. Season with salt and pepper. Stir in onion and cilantro. Keep warm.

2) Heat 1 tablespoon oil in 10-inch nonstick sauté pan over medium high heat.

3) Add tortillas 1 at a time. Cook about 30 seconds, until golden and crispy. Turn over, and cook another 30 seconds. Drain on paper towels. Continue with remaining tortillas, adding oil as needed.

4) In the same pan, cook eggs 2–3 minutes or until set, 2 at a time, sunny side up. Season with salt and pepper.

5) To serve, place each tortilla on a plate, top with 2 eggs, and spoon tomato sauce over the top.

 Tip...Serve with heated refried beans. Sauce can be made a day ahead and reheated.

raspberry orange sunshine smoothie

Prep: 10 min. **Serves:** 1

SHOPPING LIST
½ cup frozen raspberries
½ cup frozen mango chunks
1 cup vanilla Greek yogurt
½ cup orange juice
2 teaspoons honey
½ teaspoon grated orange zest

1) Place raspberries and mango in blender.

2) Combine yogurt, juice, honey and zest in 2-cup measuring cup.

3) With blender set on HIGH, add yogurt mixture through the feed tube. Stop to scrape down sides, and process until smooth.

4) Pour into a glass, and serve.

A word from Bob...

Smoothies are all the rage and so fast to make. For lots of fun, set up a "Make-Your-Own-Smoothie" station for your next brunch!

Tip...Substitute ½ teaspoon almond extract or coconut extract for honey. This recipe doubles nicely.

sparkling white sangria

Prep: 15 min. **Serves:** 6

SHOPPING LIST
1 (25-ounce) bottle chilled
    Prosecco wine
2 cups chilled ginger ale
1½ cups chilled seltzer water
1½ cups chilled orange juice,
    no pulp
1 mango, peeled and diced (1 cup)
1 orange, peeled and diced (1 cup)
1 peach, sliced into 8 wedges
    (½ cup)

1) Combine wine, ginger ale, seltzer water and juice in large punch bowl.

2) Stir in mango, orange and peach.

3) Chill, and serve.

 **Tip**...Add 1 cup brandy for more kick, and orange slices and apple slices if you like more fruit.

spicy bloody mary with shrimp skewers

Prep: 20 min. **Cook:** 10 min. **Serves:** 4

SHOPPING LIST
12 large shrimp, shelled and deveined
Salt and freshly ground black pepper to taste
1 clove garlic, peeled and halved
1 (15-ounce) can chopped tomatoes, drained
2 tablespoons lemon juice
1 tablespoon Worcestershire sauce
2 teaspoons hot sauce
¼ cup prepared horseradish sauce
1 tablespoon finely minced jalapeño pepper,
    seeds removed
¼ cup vodka
4 lemon wedges
4 short top stalks of celery with leaves

1) Place 3 shrimp each on soaked wooden skewers. Season both sides with salt and pepper.

2) Spray 10-inch sauté pan with nonstick cooking spray. Heat pan on medium-high heat, and sauté shrimp 3–4 minutes per side. Transfer to serving plate.

3) Place garlic in food processor, and pulse until evenly chopped. Add tomatoes, lemon juice, Worcestershire sauce and hot sauce, pulsing until blended.

4) Transfer mixture to bowl. Add horseradish, jalapeño and vodka. Season with salt and pepper.

5) Divide mixture into martini glasses. Place 1 skewer across each glass. Garnish with lemon wedge and celery top.

mexican chocolate sauce with cayenne pepper...p136

desserts

The crowning touch for most meals, desserts are truly the frosting on the cake. As children, we were often rewarded with these tasty treats if we ate our vegetables. Rewards await you!

Our collection of easy, tempting, indulgently delicious desserts include several twists on comfort favorites. Easy Red Velvet Cupcakes give us the mini version of this treasured cake. Maple adds a welcome new taste to everyone's beloved chocolate chip cookie. And stand back for the raves when you serve the Bread Pudding! It's even great as a midnight snack! So indulge—you are worth it!

A word from Bob...

Chocolate Lovers—we especially kept you in mind in this chapter. Most go together very quickly, and some even freeze well (like the Double Chocolate Caramel Brownies), so you will never be without your chocolate fix!

mexican chocolate sauce with cayenne pepper

Prep: 5 min. **Cook:** 10 min.
Makes: 2 cups

SHOPPING LIST
1½ cups packed brown sugar
½ cup semisweet chocolate chips
½ cup coffee
¼ cup hazelnut chocolate spread
¼ cup water
¼ teaspoon cayenne pepper
1 tablespoon vanilla extract

1) Stir sugar, chocolate, coffee, hazelnut spread, water, pepper and vanilla in 1½-quart saucepot.

2) Heat over medium-low heat 5 minutes or until melted. Simmer an additional 3 minutes.

dark chocolate key lime sauce

Prep: 5 min.　**Cook:** 10 min.　**Serves:** 6

SHOPPING LIST
¼ cup cocoa powder
1 cup sugar
¼ cup butter
½ cup sweetened condensed milk
½ teaspoon vanilla extract
1 teaspoon Key lime juice
½ teaspoon lime zest

1) Combine cocoa and sugar in small bowl.

2) Heat butter, milk and vanilla in 1½-quart saucepot over medium heat until butter melts. Add cocoa mixture, and reduce heat to low. Simmer about 5 minutes.

3) Add juice and zest. Simmer 2 minutes. Serve warm, or refrigerate for up to a week.

easy chocolate cream pie

Prep: 10 min.   **Chill:** 1 hour **Serves:** 8

SHOPPING LIST
1 (1.4-ounce) box chocolate instant pudding
⅓ cup hazelnut spread
1 prepared graham cracker crust
1 cup whipped topping
⅓ cup sour cream

1) Prepare pudding according to package directions. Mix hazelnut spread thoroughly with pudding. Spread into graham cracker crust.

2) Combine topping and sour cream. Spread on top of pudding mixture.

3) Chill 1 hour before serving.

A word from Bob...

A little coffee, cinnamon, cayenne pepper or hazelnut spread take chocolate up to a whole new level!

double chocolate caramel brownies

Prep: 10 min.   **Cook:** 50 min.   **Serves:** 12

SHOPPING LIST
1 (18¾-ounce) box brownie mix
1 (8-ounce) package mini chocolate caramel candies
½ cup prepared caramel sauce

1) Preheat oven to 325°.

2) Mix brownies according to package directions. Spread just over half the brownie mix in buttered 8x8-inch baking pan. Bake 25 minutes.

3) Stir caramel candies and sauce together.

4) Remove brownies from oven, and spread with caramel mixture. Add remaining brownie mix on top.

5) Return brownies to the oven, and cook for another 25 minutes.

6) Cool brownies completely before cutting. Brownies may appear not set when they come out of the oven, but will firm as they cool.

 Tip...If brownie mix doesn't pour smoothly in Step 4, spoon it onto caramel and swirl around.

chocolate brownie spoon bread

Prep: 15 min.   **Bake:** 40 min.

SHOPPING LIST
½ cup butter, melted
¾ cup semisweet chocolate, melted
½ cup all-purpose flour
½ cup cocoa powder
½ teaspoon baking powder
1 tablespoon instant coffee
⅛ teaspoon salt
4 eggs
1 teaspoon vanilla extract
1 cup sugar
Confectioners' sugar (optional)

1) Preheat oven to 350°. Spray 1½-quart baking dish with nonstick cooking spray.

2) Mix butter and chocolate in a medium bowl. Set aside.

3) Combine flour, cocoa, baking powder, coffee and salt in a medium bowl.

4) Beat eggs and vanilla about 6 minutes in a medium bowl. Beat in sugar until fluffy. Stir in chocolate mixture. Fold in flour mixture until combined.

5) Pour batter into prepared baking dish. Bake 40 minutes or until set but still soft in the center. Dust with confectioners' sugar, if desired.

 Tip...For an extra special dessert, top with vanilla ice cream, chocolate sauce and candied walnuts.

maple peanut butter chocolate chip cookies

Prep: 10 min.   **Chill:** 1 hour   **Bake:** 12 min.   **Serves:** 14

SHOPPING LIST

1 (18¼-ounce) package vanilla cake mix
¼ cup butter, softened
⅔ cup extra crunchy peanut butter
2 eggs
1 teaspoon maple flavoring
1 cup semisweet chocolate chips
½ teaspoon cinnamon

1) Blend cake mix with butter. Add peanut butter, eggs and flavoring, and mix well. Fold in chocolate chips and cinnamon.

2) Chill dough in refrigerator for 1 hour.

3) Drop cookies by ¼-cup measures onto parchment-lined cookie sheet, and press to flatten slightly.

4) Bake at 350° for 12 minutes or until golden. Remove, and let cool.

 Tip…Try substituting chocolate cake mix for the vanilla for a rich, chocolaty cookie.

black forest ice cream sandwich cookies

Prep: 10 min.   **Cool:** 1 hour   **Cook:** 5 min.   **Serves:** 4

SHOPPING LIST

½ cup coarsely chopped pitted cherries
1 tablespoon sugar
2 tablespoons chocolate sauce
2 cups dark cherry ice cream, softened
1 package chocolate-chunk dark chocolate cookies

1) Combine cherries and sugar in 1½-quart saucepot, and cook over medium-low heat about 5 minutes or until cherries soften. Cool completely in refrigerator.

2) Fold cherries and sauce into ice cream.

3) Place ½ cup ice cream mixture on 1 cookie. Top with another cookie. Repeat, making 3 more sandwiches.

4) Place sandwiches in single layer on cookie sheet, and freeze 1 hour before serving.

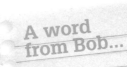

A word from Bob...

You can go nuts with this idea, literally adding nuts, fruit, marsh-mallows, chopped candy bars to your favorite ice cream and cookies. Set up an Ice Cream Sandwich Contest for your next party!

ice cream mud pie

Prep: 10 min. **Cool:** 1 hour **Chill:** 1 hour **Cook:** 10 min. **Serves:** 8

SHOPPING LIST
½ cup water
½ cup sugar
½ cup light corn syrup
¾ cup cocoa powder
⅓ cup hazelnut spread
1 cup semisweet chocolate chips
½ cup chopped hazelnuts
3 cups coffee ice cream, slightly softened, divided
1 prepared chocolate graham cracker crust

1) Combine water, sugar, corn syrup and cocoa powder in 1½-quart saucepot over medium heat. Cook about 5 minutes or until boiling. Remove from heat, and stir in hazelnut spread. Cool sauce completely in refrigerator.

2) Place chocolate chips and hazelnuts in food processor. Pulse until coarsely chopped.

3) Spread 1½ cups ice cream in graham cracker crust (return remaining ice cream to freezer for 20 minutes). Top with half chocolate chip/hazelnut mixture, pressing slightly into the ice cream. Drizzle 2 tablespoons chocolate sauce on top. Place in freezer for 30 minutes.

4) Remove pie from freezer, and spread with remaining softened ice cream, hazelnut mixture and chocolate sauce. Return to freezer for 30 minutes before serving.

Tip...If you think there are non-coffee lovers on your guest list for this dessert, use vanilla bean ice cream instead.

peach pouch pie with blueberries

Prep: 20 min.   **Cook:** 35 min.   **Serves:** 8

SHOPPING LIST

⅔ cup sugar

3 tablespoons cornstarch

4 cups peaches, pitted and sliced (about 3 pounds)

1 cup blueberries

¼ teaspoon almond extract

½ (14-ounce) package refrigerated pie crust

1) Preheat oven to 375°.

2) Stir together sugar and cornstarch in large bowl. Gently toss in peaches, blueberries and almond extract. Let stand 5 minutes.

3) Unroll one crust, and gently place in 10-inch oven-proof skillet. Spread fruit mixture evenly in crust. Fold overhanging edge to cover outer portions of filling.

4) Bake 35–40 minutes or until fruit bubbles and crust is golden brown. Cool 2 hours before serving.

caramel pear cherry almond tart

Prep: 10 min.   **Cook:** 45 min.   **Serves:** 6

SHOPPING LIST
½ cup sugar
2½ tablespoons butter
⅓ cup dried cherries
⅓ cup boiling water
½ cup sliced almonds, divided
1 large pear, peeled, cored and sliced
½ (17.3-ounce) package puff pastry sheets (1 sheet), thawed

1) Preheat oven to 400°. Combine sugar and butter in a 10-inch skillet over medium heat, and cook about 10 minutes or until medium-brown caramel forms, stirring occasionally. Remove skillet from heat, and cool completely.

2) Cover cherries with boiling water, and let stand for 5 minutes. Pour off liquid.

3) Sprinkle half the almonds on caramel. Arrange pear slices on caramel. Add cherries and remaining almonds.

4) Place pastry on top of pears, and trim excess. Tuck pastry around edges of pears. Cut 2 slits in top of pastry. Bake 30 minutes or until pastry is golden brown.

5) Remove from oven. Place large plate with raised edge over skillet. Using potholders to hold skillet and plate together, invert tart onto plate. Serve warm or at room temperature.

apple crumble pie

Prep: 30 min.   **Bake:** 35 min.   **Serves:** 8

SHOPPING LIST

1 (9-inch) deep-dish pie crust
4 medium apples, peeled, cored and thinly sliced (about 5 cups)
½ plus ⅓ cup sugar, divided
½ teaspoon cinnamon
¾ cup all-purpose flour
6 tablespoons butter, softened

1) Preheat oven to 400°. Place pie crust in 9-inch pie dish, and flute edges. Combine apples with ½ cup sugar and cinnamon in large bowl. Pour mixture into pie crust.

2) Mix remaining sugar with flour. Add butter, and mix until crumbly. Spoon mixture over apples.

3) Bake 35–40 minutes or until apples are soft and top is lightly browned.

 Tip…Serve with warm caramel sauce, whipped topping and toasted walnuts.

chocolate bourbon pecan pie

Prep: 30 min.   **Bake:** 50 min.   **Serves:** 8

SHOPPING LIST
1 (9-inch) deep-dish pie crust
¾ cup sugar
¾ cup light corn syrup
¼ cup molasses
½ cup butter
4 eggs, beaten
¼ cup bourbon whiskey
1 teaspoon vanilla extract
¼ teaspoon salt
1 cup semisweet chocolate chips
1 cup chopped pecans

1) Preheat oven to 325°. Place pie crust in 9-inch pie dish.

2) Combine sugar, corn syrup, molasses and butter in small saucepan. Cook over medium heat, stirring constantly, until butter melts and sugar dissolves. Set aside.

3) Combine eggs, whiskey, vanilla and salt. Whisk sugar mixture into egg mixture, combining thoroughly. Stir in chocolate chips and pecans. Pour mixture into pie crust.

4) Bake 50 minutes or until center is slightly soft.

Tip...Try not to overbake. Center of pie will be jiggly when properly done, but will set up during the cooling process.

cookies and cream silk cheesecake

Prep: 10 min.   **Chill:** 1 hour
Serves: 8

SHOPPING LIST
26 chocolate wafer cookies, divided
3 tablespoons butter
2 cups prepared cheesecake filling
½ cup dark-chocolate-flavored cream cheese, softened

1) Place 18 cookies and butter in food processor. Pulse until crumbs form. Press crumbs into 9-inch pie plate.

2) Cut remaining cookies in quarters. Place cheesecake filling in a medium bowl. Stir in cookies and cream cheese.

3) Spread cheesecake mixture into pie plate. Refrigerate 1 hour before serving.

Tip...If you can't find chocolate-flavored cream cheese, use regular cream cheese and 2 ounces chopped dark chocolate.

easy red velvet cupcakes with cream cheese frosting

Prep: 5 min. **Cool:** 1 hour
Cook: 18 min. **Serves:** 24

SHOPPING LIST

1 (18¼-ounce) box German chocolate cake mix
1 tablespoon white vinegar
1 tablespoon red food coloring
1 (12-ounce) container cream cheese frosting
2 cups coconut flakes

1) Preheat oven to 350°. Place liners into 24 (2½-inch) muffin-pan cups. Prepare cake mix according to package directions. Add vinegar and coloring to prepared mix. Spoon mix into muffin-pan cups, filling about two-thirds full.

2) Bake 18 minutes or until toothpick inserted in center of cupcake comes out clean. Cool cupcakes completely.

3) Frost cupcakes with frosting, and roll tops in coconut flakes.

bread pudding (pudin de pan)

Prep: 15 min. **Bake:** 40 min. **Serves:** 8

SHOPPING LIST

6 cups cubed day-old bread
3 cups milk, warmed
½ cup raisins
3 eggs, beaten
1 teaspoon vanilla
1 cup sugar
1 teaspoon cinnamon
4 tablespoons butter, melted
⅛ teaspoon salt

1) Preheat oven to 350°. Lightly butter an 8x8-inch baking pan, and set aside.

2) Soak bread in milk for 5–10 minutes in large bowl. Add raisins, and stir well.

3) Combine eggs, vanilla, sugar, cinnamon, butter and salt. Add to bread mixture, and stir well.

4) Pour bread mixture into baking pan. Bake uncovered for 40 minutes or until knife inserted near the center comes out clean.

 Tip...Serve warm, and top with your favorite dessert topping sauce.

tiramisù eggnog parfaits

Prep: 10 min. **Chill:** 4 hours **Makes:** about 6 cups

SHOPPING LIST

1 cup eggnog
1 (8-ounce) container mascarpone cheese
1 cup whipped topping
¾ cup strong coffee
¼ cup sugar
6 day-old pumpkin muffins, cut into large cubes
12 tablespoons miniature chocolate chips

1) Combine eggnog, cheese and whipped topping in a medium bowl.

2) Combine coffee and sugar in a small bowl.

3) Layer half of muffin cubes in 6 parfait glasses. Brush with half coffee mixture, and top with half of eggnog mixture, dividing evenly. Top eggnog mixture with 1 table-spoon miniature chocolate chips in each parfait glass. Repeat layers once.

4) Chill for at least 4 hours or overnight.

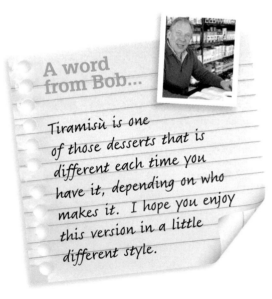

A word from Bob...

Tiramisù is one of those desserts that is different each time you have it, depending on who makes it. I hope you enjoy this version in a little different style.

banana walnut snack cake

Prep: 10 min. **Bake:** 30 min. **Serves:** 10

SHOPPING LIST
1 (18¼-ounce) package vanilla cake mix
½ teaspoon cinnamon
2 medium bananas, peeled and mashed
⅔ cup chopped walnuts
Honey

1) Preheat oven to 325°. Grease a 13x9-inch baking pan.

2) Prepare cake mix according to directions. Stir in cinnamon and bananas.

3) Pour cake mixture into prepared baking pans. Top with walnuts.

4) Bake for 30 minutes or until wooden pick inserted in center comes out clean. Remove from oven, and drizzle top of cake with honey.

 Tip...This makes a great after-school snack. Serve warm or at room temperature with a nice, cold glass of milk.

buffalo corn on the cob...p160

7 Ways, 7 Days

Seven recipes times seven variations of each one—now you can have a new creation of a treasured recipe every day of the week! We selected those comfort foods that are requested over and over, then put our very best efforts into tempting you with the results. Did you ever think of Buffalo Corn on the Cob? Or dream of a Puffy Seafood Scampi Omelet? How about yearning for Tex-Mex Cheesy Green Bean Casserole? Do you want the actual directions to Lobster Mac 'n' Cheese? Look no further!

Included in this chapter...

buffalo corn on the cob

Prep: 3 min.   **Cook and Bake:** 14 min.
Serves: 4

SHOPPING LIST
4 tablespoons unsalted butter
¼ cup buffalo hot sauce
4 ears corn, husks and silk removed
Salt and fresh ground black pepper to taste
⅓ cup crumbled blue cheese
2 teaspoons sliced chives

1) Preheat oven to 400°.

2) Melt butter with hot sauce in 3-quart skillet over medium heat. Cook for 1–2 minutes to combine flavors.

3) Add corn to skillet, and turn to coat. Season with salt and pepper. Place in oven.

4) Bake 10–12 minutes or until tender, turning halfway through cook time. Transfer to serving platter. Sprinkle blue cheese and chives on top.

Tip...Serve at your next outdoor party as a twist from traditional Buffalo wings.

italian corn on the cob

Prep: 5 min.   **Cook:** 7 min.   **Bake:** 12 min.   **Serves:** 4

SHOPPING LIST

2 tablespoons olive oil
2 garlic cloves, minced
2 tablespoons tomato paste
¼ cup water
Salt and freshly ground black pepper to taste
4 medium ears corn, husks and silk removed
6 tablespoons freshly grated Parmigiano-Reggiano cheese
2 tablespoons sliced basil

1) Preheat oven to 400°.

2) Heat oil in 3-quart oven-proof saucepan over medium heat. Add garlic, and sauté 30–60 seconds or until fragrant.

3) Whisk in tomato paste 1 minute or until combined. Whisk in water to make a thick sauce. Season lightly with salt and pepper. Remove saucepan from heat.

4) Add corn to the saucepan, turning to coat in the tomato sauce. Season with salt and pepper.

5) Place saucepan in oven, and bake 10–12 minutes or until tender, turning halfway through cook time. Brush tomato sauce all over corn. Place on serving platter. Sprinkle with cheese, and garnish with basil.

 Tip...If tomato sauce is too thick after the corn bakes, add a little water and whisk until it reaches desired consistency.

lemony corn on the cob

Prep: 5 min.   **Cook:** 18 min.   **Serves:** 4

SHOPPING LIST

4 ears corn, husks and silk removed
2 tablespoons extra virgin olive oil
Zest and juice of 1 lemon
Salt and freshly ground pepper to taste
2 tablespoons chopped parsley

1) Place corn in 5-quart saucepan. Cover completely with cold water. Bring water to a boil over high heat. Transfer from heat. Let stand covered, 12 minutes. Transfer corn to paper towels, and dry thoroughly. Place on serving platter.

2) Whisk oil, lemon zest and juice in a small bowl. Season with salt and pepper.

3) Drizzle lemon mixture over corn. Season with additional salt and pepper, if desired. Garnish with parsley.

 Tip...If cobs are not dried well, the lemon mixture is diluted and not as flavorful.

thai
corn on the cob

Prep: 8 min. **Cook:** 14 min. **Serves:** 4

SHOPPING LIST

1 tablespoon canola oil
1 tablespoon minced and peeled ginger
1 garlic clove, minced
Zest and juice of half a lime, divided
½ lime, cut into wedges
¼ cup low-sodium soy sauce
4 ears corn, husks and silk removed
Salt and freshly ground black pepper to taste
¼ cup sweetened flaked coconut

1) Place canola oil, ginger and garlic in 3-quart skillet. Sauté 1 minute over medium heat or until garlic and ginger are fragrant.

2) Stir in lime juice, and cook 30 seconds or until slightly reduced. Stir in soy sauce. Remove from heat.

3) Add corn to skillet, and turn to coat. Season with salt and pepper. Cook 10–12 minutes or until tender, turning corn halfway through cook time.

4) Top with coconut and lime zest. Place lime wedges around the platter.

Tip...Top with toasted coconut for a less sweet crunch.

bbq
corn on the cob

Prep: 4 min. **Cook:** 5 min.
Grill: 12 min. **Serves:** 4

SHOPPING LIST

2 tablespoons unsalted butter
⅓ cup barbecue sauce
Salt and freshly ground black pepper to taste
4 ears corn, husks and silk removed
1½ tablespoons sliced chives

1) Preheat grill to medium-high heat.

2) Melt butter with barbecue sauce in 1⅓-quart saucepan over medium-low heat for 5 minutes, stirring to combine. Season with salt and pepper. Transfer to a platter, and keep warm.

3) Spray grill grates with nonstick cooking spray. Place corn on grill, cover and cook 8 minutes or until tender, turning occasionally.

4) Brush corn with barbecue sauce all over, and grill 4–5 minutes or until caramelized, turning frequently. Transfer corn to serving dish. Season with salt and pepper. Garnish with chives.

fried onions and goat cheese corn on the cob

Prep: 8 min.   **Cook:** 18 min.   **Serves:** 4

SHOPPING LIST

4 ears corn, husks and silk removed
2 tablespoons extra virgin olive oil
2 tablespoons balsamic vinegar
Salt and freshly ground black pepper to taste
⅓ cup crumbled goat cheese
2 tablespoons sliced fresh basil
¾ cup French fried onions

1) Place corn in 5-quart saucepan, and cover with cold water. Bring water to a boil over high heat. Remove from heat. Cover, and let stand 12 minutes. Transfer corn to paper towels, and dry thoroughly. Place on serving platter.

2) Whisk oil and vinegar in small bowl. Season with salt and pepper.

3) Drizzle vinegar mixture over corn. Season with salt and pepper. Evenly sprinkle cheese, basil and onions on top.

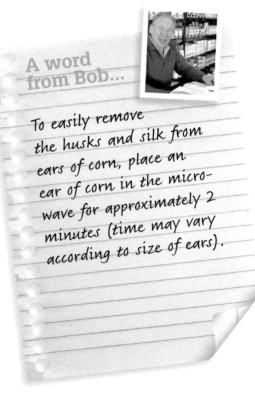

A word from Bob...

To easily remove the husks and silk from ears of corn, place an ear of corn in the microwave for approximately 2 minutes (time may vary according to size of ears).

honey butter corn on the cob

Prep: 4 min.   **Cook:** 17 min.   **Serves:** 4

SHOPPING LIST
4 tablespoons unsalted butter
2 tablespoons honey
Salt and freshly ground black pepper to taste
4 ears corn, husks and silk removed
1⅓ tablespoons sliced chives

1) Preheat grill to medium-high heat.

2) Melt butter with honey in 1¼-quart saucepan over medium-low heat. Season with salt and pepper.

3) Cook 2–3 minutes or until slightly frothy and thickened. Remove from heat, and set aside to cool slightly.

4) Grill corn covered 10–12 minutes or until tender, turning occasionally. Season with salt and pepper. Brush corn with honey mixture. Garnish with chives.

Tip...For spicy honey butter, add a pinch of cayenne pepper.

blue mac 'n' cheese...p168

best mac 'n' cheese

Prep: 15 min.   **Cook:** 45 min.
Serves: 8–10

SHOPPING LIST
6 tablespoons butter, divided
¼ cup all-purpose flour
1 teaspoon Dijon mustard
Dash of nutmeg
Dash of cayenne pepper
Dash of Worcestershire sauce
⅓ cup heavy cream
1 teaspoon chicken concentrate
⅓ cup water
¾ cup milk
3 cups shredded Cheddar cheese
2 cups shredded Swiss or Gruyère cheese
4 ounces diced Velveeta cheese
1 pound elbow pasta, cooked
1 cup panko or fresh bread crumbs

1) Melt 4 tablespoons butter in 3-quart
   sauté pan over medium heat. Stir
   in flour, and cook 3 minutes, whisking frequently. Add mustard, nutmeg,
   cayenne, Worcestershire sauce, cream,
   chicken concentrate and water. Raise
   heat slightly before adding milk. Bring
   just to a boil. Cook and stir until slightly
   thickened.

2) Remove from heat, and add cheeses,
   stirring just to blend. Toss with cooked
   pasta. Melt remaining 2 tablespoons
   butter, and toss with bread crumbs.
   Sprinkle over pasta. Bake 25–30 minutes or until hot and bubbly.

Tip...Substitute different pasta shapes
to catch the sauce – cavatappi, rotini,
shells or penne.

omg lobster mac 'n' cheese

Prep: 15 min.   **Cook:** 45 min.   **Serves:** 8–10

SHOPPING LIST

6 tablespoons butter, divided
¼ cup flour
1 teaspoon Dijon mustard
Dash of nutmeg
Dash of cayenne pepper
¾ cup white wine
¾ cup heavy cream
1 cup milk
3 cups shredded fontina cheese
2 cups shredded white Cheddar cheese
4 ounces diced Velveeta cheese
1 pound cooked pasta shells
Meat from 2 (1½-pound) steamed lobsters, diced (about 2½ cups)
1 cup panko or fresh bread crumbs
2 tablespoons chopped chives

1) Melt 4 tablespoons butter in 3-quart sauté pan over medium heat. Stir in flour, and cook 3 minutes, whisking frequently. Stir in mustard, nutmeg, cayenne, wine and cream. Raise heat slightly before adding milk. Bring just to a boil. Cook and stir until slightly thickened.

2) Remove from heat, and add cheeses, stirring just to blend. Toss with cooked pasta and lobster. Melt remaining 2 tablespoons butter, and toss with bread crumbs and chives. Sprinkle over pasta. Bake 25–30 minutes or until hot and bubbly.

Tip...You can use any cooked shellfish, such as shrimp or scallops, in this recipe instead of lobster, or you can even use a combination.

broccoli mac 'n' cheese melt

Prep: 10 min.   **Cook:** 45 min.   **Serves:** 4

SHOPPING LIST

4 tablespoons butter
2 garlic cloves, minced
¼ cup all-purpose flour
2 cups milk
½ teaspoon salt
8 ounces rigatoni
4 cups broccoli florets
1 tablespoon olive oil
2 cups shredded mozzarella cheese, divided

1) Preheat oven to 375°.

2) Melt butter in 3-quart oven-proof sauté pan over low heat. Add garlic, and cook about 2 minutes or until fragrant. Stir in flour, and cook about 2 minutes or until mixture is smooth and bubbly. Whisk in milk and salt. Cook and stir until mixture boils and thickens. Remove from heat. Cool slightly, and cover with plastic wrap directly on surface of sauce. Set aside.

3) Cook rigatoni in 5-quart stockpot, according to package directions. Add broccoli during last 2 minutes of cooking time. Drain pasta and broccoli, and toss with oil.

4) Transfer pasta mixture to sauté pan, and toss well with sauce and 1 cup cheese. Sprinkle top with remaining cheese.   Bake 15–20 minutes or until heated through and cheese is melted and bubbly.

blue mac 'n' cheese

Prep: 10 min.   **Cook:** 45 min.
Serves: 6

SHOPPING LIST

1 pound rotini or penne pasta
4 tablespoons butter
¼ cup all-purpose flour
2 cups milk
1 cup heavy cream
2 cups shredded sharp Cheddar cheese, divided
1½ cups crumbled blue cheese
½ cup julienned sun-dried tomatoes
8 slices cooked bacon, diced

1) Preheat oven to 350°.

2) Cook pasta according to package directions in 5-quart stockpot. Drain.

3) Melt butter in 3-quart oven-proof sauté pan over medium heat; sprinkle flour evenly into pan. Cook 2 minutes, whisking constantly. Add milk and cream. Bring to a boil. Cook until thickened. Remove from heat. Add 1 cup Cheddar cheese and blue cheese crumbles, stirring until cheese melts. Stir in sun-dried tomatoes and bacon. Toss with cooked pasta.

4) Transfer mixture to 3-quart baking dish, and sprinkle with remaining Cheddar cheese. Bake 25–30 minutes or until golden brown and sauce is bubbling.

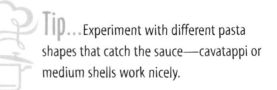 Tip...Experiment with different pasta shapes that catch the sauce—cavatappi or medium shells work nicely.

pizza mac 'n' cheese

Prep: 10 min.   **Cook:** 25 min.   **Serves:** 4

SHOPPING LIST

2 tablespoons butter

⅓ small onion, diced (⅓ cup)

1 garlic clove, minced

2 tablespoons all-purpose flour

1 cup milk

1 teaspoon dried oregano

¼ teaspoon dried red pepper flakes

3 cups mozzarella cheese, divided

1 cup pasta sauce

⅓ pound penne or rotini pasta, cooked (4 cups, cooked)

Stir-in variations:

½ cup diced pepperoni

2 links cooked Italian sausage, casings removed (about 6 ounces)

1 cup blanched broccoli florets

2 cups coarsely chopped spinach

2 cups sautéed mushrooms

1) Preheat oven to 400°.

2) Melt butter in a 3-quart oven-proof sauté pan over medium heat. Add onion, and cook about 5 minutes, until translucent. Add garlic, and cook about 1 minute, until fragrant. Whisk in flour, and cook 1 minute. Slowly whisk in milk, stirring out any clumps. Cook until thickened. Stir in seasonings. Transfer from heat.

3) Whisk in 1⅓ cups cheese, whisking until melted. Add pasta sauce and choice of desired stir-ins. Add pasta, and top with remaining cheese. Bake 15–20 minutes or until cheese is melted.

 Tip…Substitute whole-wheat pasta. Try a different serving idea: place each serving in an individual oven-proof container, and add desired stir-ins to each. Then top with cheese and bake. This recipe can easily be doubled. For extra indulgence, top with additional pepperoni, sausage or vegetable, as you would a pizza.

ranch chicken and bacon mac 'n' cheese

Prep: 10 min.   **Cook:** 30 min.   **Serves:** 4–6

SHOPPING LIST

8 ounces uncooked elbow macaroni

2 tablespoons butter

2 tablespoons all-purpose flour

1 cup milk

1 (10¾-ounce) can cream of mushroom soup

2 cups shredded Colby Jack cheese, divided

½ teaspoon onion powder

½ teaspoon garlic powder

¼ teaspoon dried dill

Kosher salt and freshly ground pepper to taste

1½ cups cooked diced or shredded chicken

8 slices cooked bacon, diced

1) Preheat oven to 375°.

2) Cook pasta according to package directions in 5-quart saucepan. Drain, and set aside.

3) Melt butter in large saucepan over medium heat. Sprinkle flour evenly into pan. Cook 2 minutes, whisking constantly. Stir milk and soup in medium bowl. Gradually stir milk mixture into saucepan. Bring to a boil, and cook 2 minutes or until thickened, whisking frequently. Remove from heat. Add 1 cup cheese, onion powder, garlic powder, dill, salt and pepper, stirring until cheese melts. Stir in pasta, chicken and bacon.

4) Transfer mixture to lightly greased 2½-quart baking dish. Sprinkle with remaining 1 cup cheese. Bake 15–20 minutes or until hot and bubbly.

mac 'n' cheese southwestern style

Prep: 10 min.   **Cook:** 45 min.   **Makes:** 2 ½ quarts

SHOPPING LIST

⅓ pound elbow pasta
½ pound ground beef
1 tablespoon chili powder
1 teaspoon ground cumin
1 (10-ounce) can tomatoes and chilies
2 tablespoons butter
2 tablespoons flour
2 cups milk
2 cups shredded sharp Cheddar cheese
8 ounces cubed Velveeta cheese
2 cups crushed tortilla chips

1) Preheat oven to 350°.

2) Cook pasta according to package directions in 5-quart stockpot. Drain and set aside.

3) Brown beef in 10-inch skillet over medium heat. Drain. Sprinkle with chili powder and cumin, and stir in tomatoes and chilies. Cook 5 minutes and set aside.

4) Melt butter in 3-quart oven-proof sauté pan over medium heat. Sprinkle flour evenly into pan. Cook 2 minutes, whisking constantly. Add milk, and bring to a boil. Cook until thickened. Transfer from heat. Add Cheddar and Velveeta, stirring until cheese melts.

5) Toss together pasta, beef mixture, and cheese mixture in sauté pan. Sprinkle with chips. Bake 25–30 minutes or until golden brown on top and sauce is bubbling.

 Tip...Substitute ground turkey for beef, or try 1½ cups cooked shredded or diced chicken for a different twist.

puffy caramelized onion, apple and brie omelet...p176

puffy omelet

Prep: 10 min. **Cook:** 18 min. **Serves:** 2

SHOPPING LIST
4 eggs, separated
2 tablespoons water
¼ teaspoon salt
⅛ teaspoon pepper
1 tablespoon butter

1) Preheat oven to 325°.

2) Beat egg whites until frothy. Add water and salt. Beat with mixer on medium high until stiff peaks form.

3) Beat egg yolks until golden. Stir in pepper. Gently fold into egg white mixture.

4) Melt butter in 10-inch skillet over low heat. Add egg mixture, smoothing surface gently with spatula. Cook without stirring for 8 minutes or until puffy and lightly browned on bottom. Transfer to oven and cook 10 minutes or until knife inserted in center comes out clean.

5) Make a shallow cut down center of omelet. Arrange choice of filling down center of omelet, fold over and slide onto serving plate.

Tip...A simple filling for this omelet is sliced fresh strawberries and softened cream cheese. Sprinkle with confectioners' sugar.

puffy pizza omelet

Prep: 15 min.   **Cook:** 32 min.   **Serves:** 2

SHOPPING LIST

8 ounces Italian sausage, thinly sliced
1 small onion, thinly sliced
⅓ green bell pepper, cored, seeded and sliced
¾ cup pasta sauce, divided
1 Puffy Omelet (page 172)
¼ teaspoon dried oregano
⅓ cup shredded mozzarella cheese

1) Cook sausage in a 10-inch skillet over medium heat about 8 minutes, until browned and cooked through. Transfer to a plate and keep warm. Add onion and bell pepper to skillet, and cook 3 minutes or until tender-crisp. Add ½ cup pasta sauce, and return sausage to skillet. Bring to a boil, reduce heat to medium low, and simmer 3 minutes or until vegetables are tender. Transfer mixture from skillet, and keep warm.

2) Prepare Puffy Omelet, adding oregano to yolks.

3) Transfer omelet from oven, arrange sausage mixture down center of omelet, and sprinkle with cheese. Fold omelet over, slide onto serving platter and top with remaining ¼ cup pasta sauce, heated.

A word from Bob...

These Puffy Omelets are easier than they look. Get the filling ready while the omelet bakes. When you take the omelet out of the oven, make the shallow cut slightly off center so when you fold the omelet over, the filling is still visible.

puffy blt omelet

Prep: 10 min.   **Cook:** 18 min.   **Serves:** 2

SHOPPING LIST

6 slices bacon, cooked and coarsely chopped
1 medium tomato, chopped
⅓ cup shredded romaine lettuce
2 cups shredded Cheddar cheese, divided
1 tablespoon mayonnaise
1 Puffy Omelet (page 172)

1) Combine bacon, tomato, lettuce, 1½ cups cheese and mayonnaise in small bowl.

2) Prepare Puffy Omelet, adding remaining ¼ cup cheese to egg yolks.

3) Transfer omelet from oven, and make the shallow cut. Arrange bacon mixture down center of omelet. Fold omelet over, and slide onto serving plate.

puffy bruschetta omelet

Prep: 15 min.   **Cook:** 18 min.   **Serves:** 2

SHOPPING LIST

1 large tomato, chopped
¼ cup chopped fresh basil, divided
2 tablespoons finely chopped onion
1 teaspoon olive oil
1 teaspoon balsamic vinegar
2 ounces goat cheese
1 Puffy Omelet (page 172)

1) Combine tomato, 2 tablespoons chopped basil, onion, oil and vinegar.

2) Prepare Puffy Omelet, adding remaining 2 tablespoons basil to egg yolks.

3) Transfer omelet from oven, and make the shallow cut. Arrange half of tomato mixture and goat cheese down center of omelet. Fold omelet over, and top with remaining tomato mixture, then slide onto serving plate.

Tip...Double the amount of the bacon mixture, and sprinkle on top of the finished omelet if you want double the impact of BLT.

puffy seafood scampi omelet

Prep: 15 min.   **Cook:** 25 min.   **Serves:** 2

4 ounces shrimp, peeled, deveined and coarsely chopped
4 ounces bay scallops
2 garlic cloves, minced
2 tablespoons butter
2 tablespoons white wine
2 slices bacon, cooked and coarsely chopped
1 Puffy Omelet (page 172)
¼ teaspoon Old Bay Seasoning

1) Toss shrimp and scallops with garlic. Melt butter in a 10-inch skillet over medium-high heat. Add shrimp mixture, and cook 5 minutes, stirring occasionally. Add wine, and cook for 2 minutes or until shrimp and scallops are cooked through. Stir in bacon. Remove from skillet, and keep warm.

2) Prepare Puffy Omelet, adding seasoning to egg yolks.

3) Transfer omelet from oven, and make the shallow cut. Arrange shrimp mixture down center of omelet. Fold omelet over, and slide onto serving plate.

puffy caramelized onion, apple and brie omelet

Prep: 15 min.   **Cook:** 34 min.   **Serves:** 2

SHOPPING LIST

2 tablespoons butter
1 medium onion, thinly sliced
¼ teaspoon salt
⅓ teaspoon sugar
1 small apple, peeled, cored and sliced
1 tablespoon chopped fresh sage, divided
1 Puffy Omelet (page 172)
2 ounces Brie cheese, thinly sliced

1) Melt butter in 10-inch skillet over medium heat. Add onion and salt, and cook about 12 minutes, until golden and very tender. Add sugar, and cook 1 minute or until caramelized. Add apple, and cook 4 minutes, until softened. Stir in 1 teaspoon sage. Transfer to platter and keep warm.

2) Prepare 1 Puffy Omelet, adding remaining sage to egg yolks.

3) Transfer omelet from oven, and make the shallow cut. Arrange onion mixture down center of omelet, and top with cheese. Fold omelet over, and slide onto serving plate.

 Tip…If you don't have fresh sage, use only 1 teaspoon dried, and add it all to the egg yolks.

puffy avocado, sweet corn and black beans omelet

Prep: 10 min.   **Cook:** 18 min.   **Serves:** 2

SHOPPING LIST
⅓ avocado, diced
⅓ cup frozen corn, thawed and drained
⅓ cup black beans, rinsed and drained
⅓ cup chopped tomato
2 tablespoons chopped cilantro, divided
2 tablespoons ranch dressing, divided
1 teaspoon tablespoon lime juice
1 Puffy Omelet (page 172)

1) Combine avocado, corn, beans, tomato, 1 tablespoon cilantro, 1 tablespoon ranch dressing and lime juice in medium bowl.

2) Prepare 1 Puffy Omelet, adding remaining 1 tablespoon cilantro and 1 tablespoon ranch dressing to yolks.

3) Transfer omelet from oven, and make the shallow cut. Arrange avocado mixture down center of omelet. Fold omelet over, and slide onto serving plate.

 Tip...For a spicier flair to this recipe, sprinkle a little chili powder or hot sauce on the avocado mixture before folding over the omelet.

pineapple upside-down cake

Prep: 10 min. **Cook:** 40 min.   **Serves:** 8

SHOPPING LIST
¼ cup butter
⅔ cup packed brown sugar
1 (20-ounce) can pineapple slices, drained, juice reserved
10 maraschino cherries
Whole pecans
1 (18¼-ounce) package yellow cake mix

1) Preheat oven to 350°.

2) Melt butter with sugar in oven-proof skillet over medium heat, stirring occasionally. Spread sugar mixture evenly over bottom of skillet.

3) Arrange pineapple slices in skillet. Center 1 cherry in each pineapple, and arrange pecans in between pineapple slices.

4) Prepare cake mix according to package directions. Pour over pineapple. Bake 40 minutes or until wooden pick inserted in center comes out clean. Invert pan over serving plate; cut and serve.

upside-down caramelized apple pie

Prep: 30 min.   **Cook:** 35 min.   **Serves:** 8

SHOPPING LIST
⅓ cup sugar
4 teaspoons cornstarch
1 teaspoon cinnamon
1 tablespoon lemon juice
1 teaspoon lemon zest
1 teaspoon ground ginger
6 apples, peeled, cored and sliced
¼ cup butter
⅓ cup brown sugar
½ (9-inch) package refrigerated pie crust (1 crust)

1) Preheat oven to 400°.

2) Stir together sugar, cornstarch, cinnamon, lemon juice, zest and ginger in a large bowl. Toss with apples.

3) Melt butter with brown sugar in a 10-inch oven-proof skillet over medium heat. Arrange apple slices in skillet. Place 1 sheet of pastry on top of apples. Press pastry to sides of skillet. Cut 3 slits in top of pastry to vent steam.

4) Bake 35 minutes or until crust is golden and apples are tender. Cool on wire rack for 10 minutes. Invert on serving plate. Spoon any remaining syrup over apples.

pear puff pie

Thaw: 40 min.   **Prep:** 30 min.
Cook: 1 hour   **Serves:** 8

SHOPPING LIST
¼ cup sugar
¼ cup cornstarch
1 teaspoon vanilla extract
1 teaspoon ground cinnamon
½ teaspoon ground nutmeg
4 cups ripe pears, peeled, cored and thinly
    sliced (about 3 pounds)
1 egg
1 tablespoon water
1 (17.3-ounce) package frozen puff pastry
    sheets (2 sheets), thawed
2 tablespoons butter, diced

1) Preheat oven to 400°.

2) Combine sugar, cornstarch, vanilla, cinnamon and nutmeg in large bowl. Add
   pears, and toss well.

3) Whisk egg and water. Roll out 1 pastry
   sheet on lightly floured surface to 12-inch
   square. Line 10-inch skillet with pastry.
   Allow 1-inch overhang, cutting off corners
   to form a circle. Brush edges with egg
   mixture. Spoon pear filling into prepared
   pastry. Dot with butter.

4) Roll out second pastry sheet to an 11-inch
   square, cutting off corners, and place on
   top of pie. Press edges together to seal.
   Cut 3 slits in top with sharp knife to vent
   steam.

5) Bake 50–55 minutes or until pastry is
   golden brown and pears are tender.

tropical banana upside-down cake

Prep: 10 min.   **Cook:** 40 min.   **Serves:** 8

SHOPPING LIST
¼ cup butter
⅔ cup brown sugar, packed
1 ripe banana, peeled and sliced
1 ripe mango, peeled and sliced
½ cup flaked coconut
1 (18¼-ounce) yellow cake mix
½ cup macadamia nuts, coarsely chopped

1) Preheat oven to 350°.

2) Melt butter and sugar over medium heat
   in a medium nonstick skillet, stirring occasionally. Spread sugar mixture evenly over
   bottom of skillet.

3) Arrange banana and mango slices over
   sugar mixture in skillet. Sprinkle with
   coconut.

4) Prepare cake mix according to package
   directions. Stir in nuts. Pour over banana-
   mango mixture. Bake 40 minutes or until
   wooden pick inserted in the center comes
   out clean.

5) Invert pan over serving plate; cut into
   pieces, and serve with vanilla ice cream.

plum crumble

Prep: 25 min. **Bake:** 40 min. **Serves:** 8

SHOPPING LIST
2 pounds plums, pitted and quartered
¼ cup packed brown sugar
2 tablespoons all-purpose flour

Topping:
1 cup all-purpose flour
½ cup sugar
½ cup packed brown sugar
½ cup rolled oats
¼ teaspoon salt
¼ pound cold unsalted butter, diced

1) Preheat oven to 375°.

2) In a large bowl combine plums, brown sugar and flour. Pour mixture into a 10-inch oven-proof skillet.

Topping:

1) Combine flour, both sugars, oats, salt, and butter in bowl of electric mixer. Mix on low speed until mixture is crumbly and is the size of peas. Sprinkle evenly over plum mixture.

2) Bake 40 minutes or until topping is brown and plums are tender.

lattice top cherry pie

Prep: 15 min. **Cook:** 30 min. **Serves:** 8

SHOPPING LIST
1 (9-inch) package refrigerated pie crust
1 cup sugar
6 tablespoons cornstarch
⅛ teaspoon salt
2 (15-ounce) cans pitted tart cherries, drained, 1 cup liquid reserved
2 tablespoons butter
¼ teaspoon almond extract

1) Preheat oven to 425°.

2) Place 1 sheet of pastry in 10-inch oven-proof skillet, pressing dough up the sides.

3) Combine sugar, cornstarch and salt in saucepan. Stir in cherry liquid, and cook over medium heat until mixture boils, stirring constantly. Remove from heat; stir in butter and almond extract until butter is melted. Stir in cherries. Pour mixture into prepared pastry.

4) Cut remaining pastry sheet into strips of equal width. Crisscross pastry strips over cherry mixture to form a lattice. Fasten ends to edge of bottom crust. Flute edge.

5) Bake 25–30 minutes or until crust is golden brown.

dark and white chocolate bread pudding pie

Prep: 20 min.   **Cook:** 1 hour   **Serves:** 8

SHOPPING LIST
2 cups semisweet chocolate chips
1 cup sugar
¼ pound unsalted butter, cubed
2 cups milk
3 eggs
1 tablespoon vanilla
2 teaspoons instant coffee powder
½ teaspoon salt
13 slices stale white bread, cut into 1-inch cubes (about 1-pound loaf)

White Chocolate Sauce:
4 ounces white chocolate chips
⅔ cup heavy cream
2 tablespoons confectioners' sugar
2 tablespoons water
1 teaspoon vanilla
2 teaspoons cornstarch
Fresh raspberries

1) Melt chocolate chips, sugar and butter in saucepan over low heat. Stir frequently until smooth.

2) Whisk milk, eggs, vanilla, coffee powder and salt, and pour over bread cubes in bowl. Toss well.

3) Fold chocolate mixture into bread mixture, and pour into 10-inch deep skillet. Bake 1 hour or until center springs back when touched. Invert pan on cooling rack. Cool 15 minutes.

4) **White Chocolate Sauce:** Melt white chocolate chips, cream and sugar in a saucepan over low heat, stirring constantly until smooth. Combine water, vanilla and cornstarch, and stir into chocolate mixture. Serve with bread pudding, and garnish with raspberries.

skillet italian chicken pot pie...p187

skillet chicken pot pie with biscuit bites

Prep: 10 min. **Cook:** 30 min. **Serves:** 4

SHOPPING LIST

1¼ pounds boneless, skinless chicken breasts,
  cut into 1-inch cubes
¼ teaspoon freshly ground black pepper
1 tablespoon canola oil
1 (12-ounce) package frozen mixed vegetables
2 (10½-ounce) cans chicken gravy
1½ cups frozen hashbrown potatoes
1 (16.3-ounce) package refrigerated large
  buttermilk biscuits
3 tablespoons grated Parmesan cheese
⅛ teaspoon crushed thyme leaves
¼ teaspoon onion powder
¼ teaspoon garlic powder

1) Preheat oven to 350°. Season chicken with
   pepper.

2) Heat oil in 9⅓-inch deep-sided skillet over
   medium-high heat. Add chicken, and cook
   about 8 minutes, until well browned on all
   sides. Transfer chicken from skillet.

3) Add vegetables, gravy and potatoes to skillet.
   Bring to a boil, stirring frequently. Reduce heat
   to medium low. Cook uncovered 5 minutes or
   until vegetables are tender-crisp, stirring occasionally. Return chicken to skillet, and heat
   until mixture is hot and bubbling.

4) Place 8 biscuits on cutting surface. Cut each
   into 3 pieces. Combine cheese, thyme, onion powder and garlic powder in small bowl.
   Dredge biscuit pieces in cheese mixture.
   Space pieces evenly on large greased cookie
   sheet. Bake 12 minutes or until golden brown.

5) Serve pot pie in bowl or ramekin topped with
   6 biscuit bites.

classic skillet chicken pot pie (pie crust topping)

Prep: 10 min.   **Cook:** 40 min.   **Stand:** 10 min.   **Serves:** 4

SHOPPING LIST

1¼ pounds boneless, skinless chicken breasts, cut into 1-inch cubes
½ teaspoon crushed Italian seasoning
¼ teaspoon freshly ground black pepper
2 tablespoons canola oil, divided
1 (8-ounce) package sliced fresh white mushrooms
1 medium onion, chopped (about ½ cup)
1 (12-ounce) package frozen mixed vegetables
1 (10¾-ounce) can condensed cream of chicken soup
1 cup water
2 teaspoons chicken or mushroom concentrate
1 tablespoon Dijon-style mustard
½ (14-ounce) package refrigerated prepared pie crust

1) Preheat oven to 425°. Season chicken with Italian seasoning and pepper.

2) Heat 1 tablespoon oil in 9⅓-inch deep-sided oven-proof skillet over medium-high heat. Add chicken, and cook until well browned on all sides, about 8 minutes. Remove chicken.

3) Heat remaining oil in skillet. Add mushrooms and onion. Cook about 4 minutes or until tender-crisp, stirring occasionally. Add vegetables, soup, water, chicken concentrate and mustard. Bring to a boil, stirring frequently. Reduce heat to medium low. Cook uncovered 5 minutes or until vegetables are tender-crisp, stirring occasionally. Return chicken to skillet, and heat until mixture is hot and bubbling.

4) Unroll pie crust on lightly floured surface, following package directions. Top skillet with crust. Press crust to chicken mixture, flute edges and trim excess. Slit pastry top.

5) Place skillet in oven. Bake 20 minutes or until crust is golden brown and baked through. Let stand 10 minutes before serving.

 Tip...Substitute 1 (8-ounce) package sliced portobello mushrooms for white mushrooms. Substitute 1 (10¾-ounce) can condensed cream of mushroom soup for cream of chicken soup. Substitute 1 (12-ounce) package frozen peas and carrots for mixed vegetables.

skillet chicken pot pie with cheese-herb biscuit topping

Prep: 10 min.   **Cook:** 35 min.   **Serves:** 4

SHOPPING LIST

1¼ pounds boneless, skinless chicken breasts, cut into 1-inch cubes
½ teaspoon crushed thyme leaves
½ teaspoon onion powder
¼ teaspoon freshly ground black pepper
1 tablespoon canola oil
1 (12-ounce) package frozen mixed vegetables
1 (10¾-ounce) can condensed cream of potato soup
1⅓ cups milk, divided
1 cup biscuit baking mix
1 egg, beaten
⅓ cup shredded Cheddar cheese
2 tablespoons chopped fresh chives
1 tablespoon chopped fresh parsley

1) Preheat oven to 400°. Season chicken with thyme, onion powder and pepper.

2) Heat oil in 9⅓-inch deep-sided oven-proof skillet over medium-high heat. Add chicken, and cook about 8 minutes, until well browned on all sides. Transfer chicken to bowl, and keep warm.

3) Add vegetables, soup and 1 cup milk to skillet. Bring to a boil, stirring frequently. Reduce heat to medium low. Cook covered 5 minutes or until vegetables are tender-crisp, stirring occasionally. Return chicken to skillet, and heat until mixture is hot and bubbling.

4) Combine baking mix, remaining ½ cup milk, egg, cheese, chives and parsley in medium bowl. Spread batter evenly over chicken mixture in skillet.

5) Place skillet in oven. Bake 30 minutes or until the biscuit topping is golden brown and baked through.

 Tip...To save time, substitute 1 (10-ounce) package refrigerated oven-roasted or grilled chicken strips for chicken breasts. Add thyme, onion powder and pepper in Step 3 with the cooked chicken strips.

skillet chicken pot pie with dumpling-style biscuits

Prep: 10 min. **Cook:** 25 min. **Serves:** 4

SHOPPING LIST

1¼ pounds boneless, skinless chicken breasts, cut into 1-inch cubes
½ teaspoon crushed thyme leaves
½ teaspoon onion powder
¼ teaspoon freshly ground black pepper
1 tablespoon canola oil
1 (12-ounce) package frozen mixed vegetables
1 (10¾-ounce) can condensed cream of chicken soup
1 cup water
2 teaspoons chicken concentrate
1 cup biscuit baking mix
⅓ cup milk
1 egg, beaten
½ cup shredded Cheddar cheese
¼ teaspoon paprika (optional)

1) Season chicken with thyme, onion powder, and pepper.

2) Heat oil in 9⅓-inch deep-sided skillet over medium-high heat. Add chicken, and cook about 8 minutes, until well browned on all sides. Transfer chicken from skillet.

3) Add vegetables, soup, water and chicken concentrate to skillet. Bring to a boil, stirring frequently. Reduce heat to medium low. Cook uncovered 5 minutes or until vegetables are tender-crisp, stirring occasionally. Return chicken to skillet, and heat until mixture is hot and bubbling.

4) Combine baking mix, milk, egg and cheese in medium bowl to form dumpling dough.

5) Drop dough by heaping tablespoons (8 total) into chicken mixture. Cook covered 10 minutes or until dough is cooked through. Sprinkle evenly with paprika, if desired. Serve chicken mixture in bowl or ramekin topped with 2 dumpling-style biscuits.

skillet italian chicken pot pie

Prep: 10 min. **Cook:** 10 min. **Serves:** 4

SHOPPING LIST

1 cup water
2 teaspoons chicken concentrate
1 (12-ounce) package frozen Italian vegetables
1 teaspoon crushed Italian seasoning
¼ teaspoon freshly ground black pepper
2 cups cooked cubed chicken
1 (15-ounce) can cannellini beans, rinsed and drained
1 (10¾-ounce) can condensed cream of chicken soup
4 tablespoons grated Parmesan cheese, divided
½ (4¾-ounce) bag oven-baked Italian toasts (10–11 pieces)

1) Heat water, chicken concentrate, vegetables, seasoning and pepper in 9⅓-inch deep-sided skillet over medium-high heat. Bring to a boil. Reduce heat to medium, and cook about 5 minutes or until vegetables are tender-crisp, stirring occasionally.

2) Stir in chicken, beans, soup and 2 tablespoons cheese. Cook covered 5 minutes or until mixture is hot and bubbling, stirring occasionally.

3) Top with toasts and sprinkle evenly with remaining 2 tablespoons cheese. Serve chicken mixture in bowl or ramekin topped with 2 Italian toasts.

—187

skillet mexican chicken pot pie

Prep: 10 min. **Cook:** 15 min. **Serves:** 4

SHOPPING LIST

1 tablespoon canola oil
½ large red bell pepper, cored, seeded and diced (about ¾ cup)
1 fresh jalapeño pepper, cored, seeded and diced (about 2 tablespoons) (optional)
1½ cups frozen whole-kernel corn
1 teaspoon ground cumin
2 cups shredded cooked chicken
1 (15-ounce) can black beans, rinsed and drained
1 (10¾-ounce) can condensed cream of chicken soup
1½ cups picante sauce
½ (2½-ounce) bag fried seasoned tortilla strips (about 1 cup)
½ cup shredded Mexican or Cheddar cheese
2 green onions, white and pale green parts, trimmed and sliced (about 2 tablespoons)

1) Heat oil in 9⅓-inch deep-sided skillet over medium-high heat. Add red pepper and jalapeño pepper, if desired. Cook 4 minutes or until tender-crisp, stirring occasionally. Stir in corn and cumin. Cook about 3 minutes or until corn is heated through, stirring frequently.

2) Stir in chicken, beans, soup and picante sauce. Bring to a boil, stirring frequently. Reduce heat to medium. Cook uncovered 5 minutes or until mixture is hot and bubbling.

3) Top with fried tortilla strips, and sprinkle evenly with cheese and onions. Serve chicken mixture in a bowl or ramekin with fried tortilla strips and additional cheese and onions, if desired.

Tip...Substitute 1 pound uncooked ground turkey or chicken for cooked chicken. To prepare, heat 1 tablespoon canola oil in skillet over medium-high heat. Add chicken or turkey, and cook about 6 minutes or until no longer pink, stirring and breaking the chicken or turkey into small pieces with a wooden spoon. Transfer from skillet and drain. Add chicken or turkey in Step 2 above.

ultimate skillet chicken pot pie

Prep: 15 min.   **Cook:** 45 min.   **Stand:** 10 min.   **Serves:** 4

SHOPPING LIST

3 tablespoons butter

1 large onion, chopped (about 1 cup)

2 medium potatoes, peeled and diced (about 1½ cups)

2 stalks celery, sliced ½-inch thick (about 1 cup)

2 medium carrots, peeled and sliced ½-inch thick (about 1 cup)

1 teaspoon crushed thyme leaves

⅓ teaspoon salt

¼ teaspoon freshly ground black pepper

2 tablespoons brandy or cognac

2 tablespoons all-purpose flour

1 cup water

2 teaspoons chicken concentrate

¾ cup milk

2 cups shredded cooked chicken

1 cup frozen peas

4 tablespoons chopped fresh parsley, divided

½ (17.3-ounce) package frozen puff pastry, thawed (1 sheet)

1 egg

1 tablespoon water

1) Preheat oven to 425°.

2) Melt butter in 9⅓-inch deep-sided oven-proof skillet over medium-high heat. Add onion, potatoes, celery, and carrots. Cook about 10 minutes or until vegetables are tender-crisp, stirring occasionally. Add thyme, salt and pepper. Carefully stir in brandy, and cook 30 seconds. Gradually stir in flour, and cook 2 minutes, stirring constantly. Gradually stir in water. Add chicken concentrate and milk. Bring mixture to a boil. Reduce heat to medium, and cook 2 minutes or until thickened, stirring constantly.

3) Stir in chicken, peas, and 2 tablespoons parsley. Heat chicken mixture until hot and bubbling. Remove skillet from heat.

4) Unfold pastry sheet on a lightly floured surface. Cut pastry crosswise into 6 strips (1½ inches wide). Weave a lattice pattern over chicken mixture in skillet. Trim excess pastry. Beat egg and water in small bowl. Brush pastry top evenly with egg mixture.

5) Place skillet in oven. Bake 25 minutes or until chicken mixture is hot and bubbling and pastry is golden brown and baked through. Let stand 10 minutes before serving. Garnish with remaining 2 tablespoons parsley.

 Tip...Substitute cooked, cubed chicken or turkey for shredded chicken, or substitute 1 (10-ounce) package refrigerated oven-roasted or grilled chicken strips for shredded chicken.

easy green bean casserole

Prep: 10 min. **Cook:** 10 min. **Serves:** 6

SHOPPING LIST

4 tablespoons unsalted butter, divided
1 small sweet onion, finely chopped
1 tablespoon all-purpose flour
1¼ cups milk or water
1 cup shredded Cheddar cheese
1 tablespoon chicken concentrate
¾ pound green beans, trimmed, halved,
  and blanched
1 cup crushed butter crackers

1) Preheat oven to 400°.

2) Melt butter in deep 10-inch nonstick
   oven-proof skillet over medium heat.
   Cook onion 4 minutes or until just starting to brown, stirring occasionally.
   Sprinkle with flour, and cook 1 minute,
   stirring frequently. Gradually whisk in
   milk. Bring to a boil, and cook about 1
   minute or until thickened.

3) Stir in cheese and chicken concentrate.
   Cook until cheese is melted. Add beans,
   and stir to coat. Sprinkle with cracker
   crumbs, and dot with remaining 2 tablespoons butter.

4) Bake uncovered in skillet 15 minutes or
   until crumbs are golden brown.

tex-mex cheesy green bean casserole...p193

savory bacon and blue cheese green bean casserole

Prep: 10 min.   **Cook:** 35 min.   **Serves:** 6

SHOPPING LIST

2 tablespoons olive oil
1 small sweet onion, finely chopped
1 (8-ounce) package sliced mushrooms
1 tablespoon all-purpose flour
1⅓ cups milk
½ cup crumbled blue cheese
1 tablespoon chicken concentrate
⅛ teaspoon freshly ground black pepper
1 teaspoon dried thyme leaves
1 (12-ounce) green beans, trimmed and halved
½ cup crushed round butter crackers
2 tablespoons finely chopped crisp bacon or bacon bits

1) Preheat oven to 350°.

2) Heat oil in deep 10-inch nonstick skillet over medium heat. Cook onion and mushrooms 6 minutes or until just starting to brown, stirring occasionally. Sprinkle with flour, and cook 1 minute, stirring frequently. Gradually whisk in milk. Bring to a boil, and cook about 1 minute or until thickened. Stir in cheese, chicken concentrate, pepper and thyme. Cook until cheese is melted. Stir in beans. Simmer 5 minutes or until beans are tender.

3) Transfer to 11x7-inch shallow casserole dish, and sprinkle with cracker crumbs. Top with bacon.

4) Bake uncovered 20 minutes or until crumbs are golden brown and green bean mixture is bubbling.

green bean and tomato casserole with whole-grain crunch topping

Prep: 10 min.   **Cook:** 30 min.   **Serves:** 6

SHOPPING LIST

2 tablespoons olive oil
1 (12-ounce) package frozen green beans, trimmed and halved
½ cup chopped red onion
2 garlic cloves, finely chopped
2 teaspoons all-purpose flour
⅓ cup milk
1 cup cherry tomatoes, halved
⅛ teaspoon freshly ground black pepper
½ cup crunchy whole-grain pecan cereal

1) Preheat oven to 350°.

2) Heat oil in deep 10-inch nonstick skillet over medium heat. Cook beans and onion 6 minutes or until tender-crisp, stirring occasionally. Sprinkle with flour and cook 1 minute, stirring frequently. Gradually whisk in milk. Bring to a boil, and cook about 30 seconds or until thickened. Reduce heat to low, and stir in tomatoes and black pepper. Cover and cook 3–4 minutes or until beans are tender.

3) Transfer to 11x7-inch shallow casserole dish, and sprinkle with cereal.

4) Bake uncovered 15 minutes or until cereal is golden brown and green bean mixture is bubbling.

Tip…Skip the casserole dish and leave the beans in the skillet—one less dish to wash!

tex-mex cheesy green bean casserole

Prep: 5 min. **Cook:** 25 min. **Serves:** 6

SHOPPING LIST

¾ cup milk

1 (10¾-ounce) can condensed cream of mushroom soup

1 cup refrigerated prepared pico de gallo or salsa

¼ teaspoon freshly ground black pepper

1 (12-ounce) package frozen green beans, thawed

2 cups shredded Pepper Jack cheese, divided

1 cup crushed yellow or white corn tortilla chips

1) Preheat oven to 350°.

2) Combine milk, soup, pico de gallo, pepper, beans, and 1½ cups cheese in 11x7-inch shallow casserole dish.

3) Bake uncovered 20 minutes or until green bean mixture is bubbling. Sprinkle with chips and remaining ½ cup cheese, and bake 5 minutes or until cheese is melted.

cheesy green beans with mushrooms

Prep: 10 min. **Cook:** 30 min. **Serves:** 6

SHOPPING LIST

2 (16-ounce) bags frozen whole green beans, cooked and drained
3 tablespoons butter
8 ounces sliced mushrooms
¼ cup chopped onion
3 tablespoons all-purpose flour
1¼ cups milk
1 cup shredded Cheddar cheese
1 tablespoon Dijon mustard
1 tablespoon olive oil
¼ cup panko bread crumbs

1) Preheat oven to 350°. Spray 2-quart baking dish with cooking spray. Place beans in dish.

2) Melt 3 tablespoons butter in saucepan over medium heat. Stir in mushrooms and onion. Cook until vegetables are tender. Stir in flour, and cook 1 minute.

3) Slowly add milk, and cook until thickened, stirring constantly. Stir in cheese and mustard. Pour mushroom mixture over beans.

4) Heat oil in small skillet over medium heat. Stir in bread crumbs, and cook until golden brown, stirring constantly. Sprinkle over bean mixture. Bake for 30 minutes or until hot.

green beans alfredo

Prep: 10 min. **Cook:** 30 min.
Serves: 6–8

SHOPPING LIST

2 (16-ounce) bags frozen French-cut green beans, cooked and drained
1 (15-ounce) jar "light" or regular Alfredo sauce
3 slices bacon, cooked and crumbled (about ¼ cup)
1 cup fat-free restaurant-style seasoned croutons

1) Preheat oven to 350°. Spray 2-quart baking dish with nonstick cooking spray.

2) Pour beans in bottom of baking dish. Pour sauce over beans. Sprinkle with bacon and croutons.

3) Bake 30 minutes or until hot.

green beans and potato bake

Prep: 15 min.   **Cook:** 30 min.   **Serves:** 6

SHOPPING LIST

8 small red potatoes (about ½ pound)
1 (16-ounce) bag frozen Italian-cut or whole green beans
1 tablespoon olive oil
2 garlic cloves, chopped
1 (15-ounce) can Italian-seasoned diced tomatoes
½ teaspoon salt
¼ teaspoon ground pepper
1 cup shredded mozzarella cheese
½ cup grated Parmesan cheese

1) Preheat oven to 350°.

2) Cover potatoes with water in large saucepan. Bring to a boil over medium-high heat. Lower heat to medium, and cook covered for 10 minutes. Add beans to pot. Cook about 8 minutes, until potatoes and beans are tender. Drain.

3) Cool potatoes, and slice thin.

4) Heat olive oil in skillet over medium heat. Cook garlic 30 seconds or until fragrant. Add tomatoes, salt and pepper. Heat through.

5) Transfer beans to 2-quart baking dish. Layer potatoes over beans. Pour tomato mixture over potatoes, and top with cheeses. Bake for 30 minutes or until hot.

baked cornbread, chicken and rice

Prep: 15 min.   **Cook:** 45 min.
Serves: 4–6

1 cup long-grain rice
1⅓ cup milk, divided
1 (15-ounce) can cream-style corn
¼ cup dried cranberries
1⅓ teaspoons salt, divided
¼ teaspoon sage
¼ teaspoon celery seeds
¼ teaspoon pepper
1¼ pounds boneless, skinless chicken
  thighs
1 (8.5-ounce) package cornbread
  muffin mix
1 egg

1) Preheat oven to 375°.

2) Combine rice, 1 cup milk, corn, cranberries and 1 teaspoon salt in 5-quart casserole or oven-proof saucepan. Combine remaining salt, sage, celery seeds, and pepper in small dish.

3) Place chicken on top of rice mixture, and season with sage mixture.

4) Combine muffin mix with remaining ⅓ cup milk and egg. Spread muffin mixture on top of chicken. Cover, and bake covered 45 minutes.

Tip...Serve with garden salad for a tasty meal.

cheesy broccoli baked chicken and rice

Prep: 15 min. **Cook:** 45 min. **Serves:** 4

SHOPPING LIST

1 (10½-ounce) can condensed cheese soup
1½ cups milk
1 cup long-grain rice
1 cup finely chopped broccoli
1¼ pounds boneless, skinless chicken thighs
½ teaspoon salt
¼ teaspoon pepper
¼ teaspoon garlic powder
1 cup seasoned bread crumbs
2 tablespoons Parmesan cheese
2 tablespoons melted butter

1) Preheat oven to 375°.

2) Combine soup, milk, rice and broccoli in 3-quart casserole or oven-proof saucepan.

3) Place chicken on top of rice mixture. Season chicken with salt, pepper and garlic powder.

4) Mix bread crumbs and cheese with butter. Sprinkle bread crumb mixture over chicken.

5) Cover, and bake covered 45 minutes.

pesto baked chicken and rice

Prep: 15 min.   **Cook:** 45 min.   **Serves:** 4

SHOPPING LIST

1 (10½-ounce) can cream of chicken soup
1¼ cups water
1 cup long-grain rice
1 cup chopped zucchini
1 cup chopped red and green bell peppers
1 (½-ounce) package pesto sauce mix
2 tablespoons olive oil
1¼ boneless, skinless chicken thighs

1) Preheat oven to 375°.

2) Combine soup, water, and rice in 3-quart casserole or oven-proof saucepan. Add zucchini and bell peppers.

3) Combine pesto mix and oil in bowl. Add chicken to pesto mixture, and coat thoroughly. Place chicken on top of rice mixture.

4) Cover, and bake covered 45 minutes.

baked chicken and rice

Prep: 15 min.   **Cook:** 45 min.   **Serves:** 4

SHOPPING LIST

1 (1.8-ounce) package leek soup mix
1¼ cups milk
1¼ cups water
⅓ cup chopped carrots
½ cup chopped celery
1 cup long-grain rice
1¼ pounds boneless, skinless chicken thighs
½ teaspoon salt
¼ teaspoon pepper
¼ teaspoon celery salt

1) Preheat oven to 375°.

2) Place soup mix, milk, and water in 3-quart casserole or oven-proof pot. Add carrots, celery and rice. Stir until thoroughly mixed. Top with chicken thighs. Season chicken with salt, pepper and celery salt.

3) Cover, and bake 45 minutes.

Tip…Serve with a side salad for a wonderful anytime meal.

baked chicken and risotto with peas

Prep: 20 min. **Cook:** 50 min. **Serves:** 6

SHOPPING LIST

6 boneless, skinless trimmed chicken thighs (1¾ pounds)
Salt and freshly ground black pepper to taste
2 tablespoons olive oil
1 medium onion, chopped (1 cup)
2 cups Arborio rice or other short-grain rice
3½ cups water
2 tablespoons chicken concentrate
1 (14½-ounce) can diced tomatoes
1 dried bay leaf
1 cup frozen peas, thawed
1 (4-ounce) bottle sliced sweet pimentos, drained

1) Preheat oven to 400°.

2) Heat oil in 5-quart nonstick oven-proof saucepan over medium-high heat. Season chicken on both sides with salt and pepper. Add chicken to saucepan. Cook about 5 minutes per side or until lightly browned.

3) Transfer chicken from saucepan, and add onion. Cook onion 5 minutes or until tender-crisp, stirring frequently. Add rice, and cook about 2 minutes or until glossy, stirring occasionally. Season rice mixture with salt and pepper.

4) Add water, chicken concentrate, tomatoes and bay leaf. Raise heat to medium high, and bring to a boil. Transfer saucepan to oven, and cook 25 minutes.

5) Transfer from oven, and fluff rice mixture with a fork. Stir in peas and pimentos. Cover saucepan, and let stand for 5 minutes.

Tip...Add a pinch of saffron.

asian baked chicken and rice

Prep: 40 min.　**Cook:** 45 min.　**Serves:** 4

SHOPPING LIST

1¼ pounds boneless, skinless chicken thighs

¼ cup Asian toasted sesame salad dressing or marinade

1 (11.8-ounce) can coconut water

1 cup jasmine rice

½ cup water

½ teaspoon salt

1 (12-ounce) package frozen vegetables (broccoli, carrots, sugar peas and water chestnuts)

Salt and cracked black pepper to taste

1) Preheat oven to 375°.

2) Place chicken in bowl, and add dressing. Stir to thoroughly coat chicken. Let stand at least 30 minutes.

3) Place coconut water, rice, water and salt in greased 3-quart casserole; stir. Layer vegetables on top of rice mixture.

4) Place undrained chicken thighs on top of vegetables. Season with cracked pepper and salt. Cover, and bake 45 minutes.

 Tip...Serve with soy sauce.

baked chicken with red beans and rice

Prep: 10 min. **Cook:** 45 min. **Serves:** 4

SHOPPING LIST
1 (1¼-ounce) package mild chili seasoning mix, divided
1 (15-ounce) can red beans, undrained
1 (15-ounce) can diced tomatoes
1 cup rice
1½ cups water
½ teaspoon salt
1¼ pounds boneless, skinless chicken thighs

1) Prcheat oven to 375°.

2) Reserve 2 teaspoons seasoning mix.

3) Combine beans, tomatoes, rice, water, salt and remaining seasoning mix in a 3-quart casserole or oven-proof saucepan. Place chicken on top of rice mixture. Season chicken with reserved 2 teaspoons seasoning.

4) Cover, and bake 45 minutes.

 Tip...Top with cornbread muffin mix, and bake the bread in same dish.

about
the author

Bob Warden is a renowned television cooking celebrity, kitchenware developer and cookbook author. His newest venture, Great Chefs International, includes a TV show and a variety of new cookbooks as well as the premiere of Great Flavors®, a collection of concentrated stocks, sauces, and seasonings. In a highly productive print career, Bob has published eight customer top-rated, five-star cookbooks. They include *Quick and Easy Pressure Cooking, The Ninja Master Prep Cookbook, The Ninja Master Prep Professional Cookbook, The Ultimate Bulk Buying Cookbook, Best of the Best* ***cook's essentials*** and the ultimate go-to reference for pressure cooking, *Bob Warden's Slow Food Fast*. The sequel, *Great Food Fast*, has sold more than 100,000 copies so far in 2012.

pantry list

Shop for these items, or keep them on hand to prepare all the recipes in this cookbook.

BAKING ITEMS
almond extract
baking mix
baking powder
brown sugar
brownie mix
cheesecake filling
chocolate graham cracker crust
cocoa powder
coconut flakes
confectioners' sugar
corn syrup, light
cornmeal
cornstarch
cream cheese frosting
flour
German chocolate cake mix
graham cracker crust
mini chocolate chips
molasses
red food coloring
semisweet chocolate chips
sugar
sweetened condensed milk
vanilla cake mix
vanilla extract
yellow cake mix
walnuts

BREADS
baguettes
ciabatta rolls
cinnamon swirl bread
croutons
herb-seasoned stuffing
Italian bread
Italian-style hoagie rolls
Italian toasts
pumpernickel swirl bread
round bread loaf
rye bread
tortillas, corn, flour
white bread

CHEESE
blue cheese
Brie cheese
Cheddar cheese
Colby Jack cheese
cream cheese
dark chocolate cream cheese
feta cheese
Fontina
goat cheese
Gruyère cheese
mozzarella, fresh
Parmesan, grated, shaved, shredded
Pecorino Romano
pepper Jack cheese
ricotta cheese
Swiss cheese, sliced
Velveeta®
white Cheddar

DAIRY SECTION
biscuits
butter, salted, unsalted
cream, heavy
eggnog
eggs
Greek yogurt, plain
mascarpone cheese
milk
pie crust
pizza dough
sauerkraut, fresh
skim milk
sour cream
yogurt, plain

FRESH HERBS
basil
bay leaves
chives
cilantro
oregano
parsley
rosemary
sage
tarragon
thyme

FRESH PRODUCE
apples
arugula
asparagus
avocados
bananas
bell peppers, green, red
blueberries
broccoli florets
carrots, regular, baby
cauliflower
celery
cherries
corn
cucumbers
eggplant
garlic
ginger
grape tomatoes
green beans
green onions
jalapeño peppers
kale
leeks
lemons
limes
mangoes
mushrooms, button, shiitake, baby bella caps
Napa cabbage
onions, red, sweet, Vidalia
oranges
peaches
pears
plums
plum tomatoes
potatoes, red, sweet
raspberries
radicchio
radish
romaine lettuce
salad greens
serrano chile peppers
shallots
spaghetti squash
spinach, baby
tomatoes
zucchini

FROZEN FOODS
coffee ice cream
dark cherry ice cream
hash brown potatoes
Italian vegetables
mango chunks
mixed vegetables
phyllo dough
peas
pie crust (deep-dish)
puff pastry sheets
raspberries
spinach, chopped
Texas toast
vegetable blend – broccoli, carrots, sugar peas, water chestnuts
whipped topping

FRUIT, CANNED, DRIED AND JUICE
cherries, dried, maraschino, tart
coconut
cranberries
dates, pitted
Key lime juice
lemon juice
lime juice
orange juice
pineapple slices
raisins, dried, golden

MEATS, POULTRY AND FISH
bacon
bay scallops
beef chuck
beef chuck steaks
beef, ground
bulk sausage
chicken, cooked
chicken, ground
chicken breasts, boneless, skinless
chicken thighs, bone-in
chicken thighs, boneless, skinless
chorizo
crab, fancy lump, canned

pantry list...(continued).

MEATS, POULTRY AND FISH (cont.)

Flat Iron steak
ham steak
Italian sausage, sweet
lobsters, cooked
pancetta
pepperoni
pork chops
pork, ground
pork tenderloin
prosciutto
shrimp
skirt steak
salmon fillets
tuna, canned
turkey, deli sliced

NUTS

almonds, sliced
hazelnuts
pecans
pine nuts
pistachios

OTHER

Alfredo sauce
anchovy paste
applesauce
apricot preserves
Asian toasted sesame seed salad dressing
balsamic vinegar
barbecue sauce
black beans
bread crumbs, regular, panko, seasoned
buffalo hot sauce
butter crackers
canola oil
capers
cannellini beans
caramel sauce
chick peas
chicken gravy
chili oil
chili seasoning mix
chocolate chunk cookies
chocolate instant pudding
chocolate sauce
chocolate wafer cookies

cider vinegar
coconut water
coffee
corn, whole-kernel, cream-style
cornbread
cornbread muffin mix
crackers, round snack
cumin
Dijon mustard
fish sauce
French fried onions
Great Northern beans
hazelnut spread
hominy
honey
horseradish sauce
hot sauce
instant coffee
kalamata olives
kidney beans
mayonnaise
mini chocolate caramel candies
oats, rolled
olive oil
pasta sauce
peach mango salsa
peanut butter, extra-crunchy
pesto
pesto sauce mix
picante sauce
pico de gallo
pimento
pita chips
plum tomatoes
porcini mushrooms, dried
pretzel crisps
pumpkin bread or muffins
ranch dressing
red beans
red lentils
red wine vinegar
rice wine vinegar
roasted red peppers
Russian dressing
salsa
sauerkraut, canned
soy sauce, reduced sodium
sun-dried tomatoes
sweet chili sauce
tamari sauce

tomatoes, crushed, diced, fire-roasted, Italian seasoned, chopped
tomatoes and chiles
tomato paste
tomato sauce
tortilla chips
tortilla strips, fried, seasoned
Thousand Island dressing
vegetable oil
white beans
white chocolate chips
white corn chips
white pepper
white vinegar
white wine vinegar
whole-grain pecan cereal
Worcestershire sauce

PASTA, RICE, GRAINS AND NOODLES

Arborio rice
couscous
elbow macaroni
farro
jasmine rice
long-grain white rice
mini pasta
noodles
pasta shells
penne
red quinoa
rigatoni
rotini
spaghetti

SOUPS AND SOUP MIXES

chicken broth
condensed cheese soup
condensed cream of chicken soup
condensed cream of mushroom soup
condensed cream of potato soup
condensed French onion soup
French onion soup mix
leek soup mix

SPICES, SEASONINGS AND FLAVORINGS

ancho chili powder
black pepper

cannellini beans
caraway seeds
cayenne pepper
celery seeds
chili powder
chipotle chili powder
cinnamon, ground
cinnamon sticks
cloves, whole
cumin, ground
coriander, ground
dill, dried
ginger, ground
garlic powder
Great Flavors® Beef Concentrate
Great Flavors® Chicken Concentrate
Great Flavors® Mushroom Concentrate
Great Flavors® Vegetable Concentrate
herbes de Provence
hot pepper flakes
Old Bay Seasoning
onion, dried, minced
onion powder
oregano
maple flavoring
nutmeg
paprika, smoked, regular
pepper, black
poultry seasoning
red pepper, ground
red pepper flakes
salt
sea salt

WINE, SPIRITS, AND OTHER DRINKS

bourbon whisky
brandy
cognac
ginger ale
Prosecco wine
red wine
seltzer water
tawny port
tequila
vodka
white wine

index

main dishes

salads

7 ways, 7 days

CHICKEN AND RICE

CORN ON THE COB

soups